MODERN
FILE
SCRIPTS

TRISTANA

a film by
Luis Buñuel

translated by Nicholas Fry

Simon and Schuster, New York

All rights reserved including the right
of reproduction in whole or in part in any form
English translation copyright © 1971 by Lorrimer Publishing Limited
Original French language edition entitled *Tristana*
© 1971 by L'Avant-Scène du Cinéma
Published by Simon and Schuster
Rockefeller Center, 630 Fifth Avenue
New York, New York 10020
First Printing

General Editor: Sandra Wake

SBN 671-21078-5
Library of Congress Catalog Card Number: 70-163104

This edition is for sale only in the United States of America,
its territories, possessions, protectorates, and places mandated to it,
the Philippines and the Dominion of Canada

Manufactured in Great Britain by Villiers Publications Ltd,
London NW5

CONTENTS

A Note on this Edition 4
Introduction by J. Francisco Aranda 5
Credits 12
Cast 13
Tristana 15

A NOTE ON THIS EDITION

The present publication is based on the French script published by l'Avant-Scène du Cinéma, which was itself based on Luis Buñuel's original script and supplemented by material obtained from a shot-by-shot viewing of the French-dubbed film. This version was then translated into English and combined with a transcript of the Spanish dialogue. The result was then finally checked with the English subtitled print in order to make it as accurate a rendering as possible of the film which the English or American spectator will see on the screen.

The English print of the film was found to be seven minutes shorter than the French version and scenes which were either omitted from the English subtitled version or cut in the original editing, as well as parts of the original script which were not shot, are indicated in this script by square brackets.

The photographs are taken from production stills and therefore occasionally do not correspond exactly to the text.

Our thanks are due to Ivo Jarosy of The Academy Cinema for allowing us to view the film. Stills are by courtesy of l'Avant-Scène du Cinéma, The Academy Cinemas, The British Film Institute and J. Francisco Aranda.

INTRODUCTION
by
J. Francisco Aranda

In festivals all over the world, *Tristana* has been classified as one of the two or three best films of the year. It has a comparatively straightforward story and is one of Buñuel's less spectacular or provocative films. The reason for its success can only lie in the abilities of its creator. Luis Buñuel is considered one of the great film directors of our time. But it has seldom been pointed out that he is an even better scriptwriter. This quality is combined with a minute attention to detail. The sudden close-ups of trivial objects which gain an unexpected significance, the gesture of an actor which is unnecessary for the development of the narrative, but which at once reveals his feelings with an almost psychoanalytical precision, and the final editing (which Buñuel always does or controls himself): all these transform the material into something individual, a fascinating affirmation of his personality.

How the script was born

In 1961, after 25 years in exile, Buñuel had directed *Viridiana* in his homeland and he wanted to continue working there, 'making films for Spanish audiences' he told us. *Viridiana* was, of course, forbidden in Spain after having won the Grand Prix at the Cannes festival, and it still remains banned there. This is not what Buñuel wanted, although malicious suggestions have been made to the contrary. 'Of course, I knew how subversive my film was, but I expected that it would be accepted (perhaps after the cutting of 3 or 4 shots) as a strong story.' Being unfamiliar with the present situation in his country, he had miscalculated, and next time he wanted to hit the right formula.

A new production company in Madrid had offered him a chance. After studying a number of Buñuel's synopses and suggestions, it was finally decided that *Tristana* would be the best: Spanish in character and in the problems it dealt with, not too complicated. The author of the original book — a Liberal of the end of the past century — was beginning to be officially praised. His work, till recently considered dangerous, was now acceptable with the 'new look' the Government wanted to give to their future activities.

Benito Pérez Galdós (1843–1920) was being rediscovered, partly thanks to Buñuel's adaptation of *Nazarin* (1958). After having enjoyed great success during his life, he was despised in the Twenties as an over-descriptive writer, who produced dozens of fat books influenced by literary Naturalism. But Buñuel had read and loved all his works during his years as a student. He liked the way Galdós grasped the essence of the national middle class and defined human types. Galdós' work has clearly influenced Buñuel's own conceptions, although he has adapted it to his own ideas and interpreted it according to his surrealist viewpoint. He has sometimes replaced Galdós' moral conclusions by his own. Buñuel worked this way on *Angel Guerra, Doña Perfecta* and *Tristana*, a novel of 80 pages written by Galdós three years before *Nazarin*. Today Galdós is considered Spain's greatest writer after Cervantes, and Buñuel has declared: 'He is as great as Dostoevsky or Balzac.'

'*Tristana* is Galdós' worst book, but it allows me to observe some aspects of Spanish life and customs in which I am interested,' Buñuel told us. When we said, in 1965, how sorry we were that he could not do other more brilliant projects, he replied: 'What's the difference? I'll go on working with the subjects I have always enjoyed: religion and eroticism' (and, although he did not say it, 'their mutual relationship'). 'You know that I could make a Buddhist film of the life of Christ.' This does not mean that Buñuel obsessively produces the same conclusions from any story, but rather that he can extract from certain stories a few themes which he investigates in all his films. The script of *Tristana* was written in Mexico with Julio Alejandro, a Spanish writer who had emigrated there after having a play put on by the National ('Español') theatre. It must be stressed, however, that Buñuel's collaborators do little more than write down the script as he conceives it, after discussing some details and polishing the dialogue.

The adaptation

The script follows the plot of the book, particularly until the arrival of Horacio. Buñuel saw that the outmoded side of the novel lay in the development of the relationship between the two lovers; he transformed it, shortening the role of the young hero. At the same time all the other characters were greatly intensified: Tristana becomes much harder and more embittered than in the book. Don Lope embodies all the contradictions of a provincial gentleman who wants to appear progressive and atheistic, but is tied to the traditional, almost feudal, habits and social privileges of the nineteenth-century bourgeoisie. Towards the end of the film Don Lope becomes more decrepit than in the book. His transformation into a more sentimental man is mixed with resignation and hypocrisy. The servant, Saturna, becomes more vivid and her son, who hardly appears in the book, is brought in by Buñuel for the sake of a definition of adolescent problems (which range from masturbation to labour strikes). Then, in a stroke of genius, the action is transferred from the end of the nineteenth century to the late Twenties, the time of the first military dictatorship in Spain, which Buñuel knew so well. An equally successful transposition had been made by him in *Le journal d'une femme de chambre* (1963), a work that is parallel in many ways to *Tristana*. In addition, the location had to be changed from Madrid, as the capital no longer displayed the same social and moral conditions as in the book: these conditions were, however, still to be found in a less cosmopolitan milieu. The town chosen was Toledo, only 50 miles away from Madrid. Galdós had described it as a fascinating jewel of art, a helpless relic, a town with no future. During his student years (1919–1924), Buñuel used to go there with his friends in search of the world of Galdós and he often lunched at the 'Bloody Inn' (Posada de la Sangre). Thus he was able to study the old Spanish society from the inside, where it was at its most obvious. All this must have contributed to the present work: the *Nazarin* and *Tristana* scripts are better than the original books!

It took a lot of work and skilful manipulation to complete the script. In the last seven years Buñuel rewrote it three more times. A detailed comparison between the first and the fourth treatment, though a long and laborious process, would lead us to a valuable understanding of Buñuel's method of work. It is rather painful, highly selective, much less intuitive and spontaneous than film critics generally believe. The plot became more and more condensed, meaningful, furiously corrosive. Quite a few juicy sequences were eliminated, such as the church scene, when Tristana goes to confess. A disillusioned, ageing, unmarried creature, she becomes an over-pious woman. She tells the priest how many sins she commits, how many horrible temptations she falls into and the severe penances she imposes on herself. The priest, very alarmed, warns her: 'My daughter, by inflicting such severe punishments on yourself, are you not perhaps committing the additional sin of arrogance?' The priest has guessed that Tristana's sexual frustration is leading her into abysses of perversion and masochism. Like all the priests portrayed by Buñuel throughout the admirable gallery of his films, this one is much more clever than he actually looks and pretends to be. This is of course how most Spanish priests are, and the Freudian sexual deviation of Tristana is often characteristic of the Latin woman inside the Catholic religion.

At first one might regret the omission of such a sequence. Like all Buñuel's best scenes, it is both dramatic and exhilarating. But this kind of stuff belongs to the time of masterpieces like *El* (1952). Buñuel no longer indulges in such derision. Tristana's metamorphosis towards the end of the film is calculated in such a way as to make her deviation easily deduced.

In face of such a restrained, anti-rhetorical work of art, the script was approved by the Censors without cuts.

The filming

With the production carefully planned and the settings and abundant exteriors chosen, the film was ready to start early in 1964. Suddenly official permission for shooting was refused. Both the Censors and Buñuel had been most suspicious: the Censors were afraid of being tricked by the film director (as in *Viridiana*); Buñuel wanted to make the film acceptable to the authorities, without making it seem a gesture of surrender from a recent exile. The affair was closed. However, the producers had invested a lot of hopes and money in the enterprise and did not give up. Early in 1969 they estimated that the production was again possible, convinced Buñuel to come back to Madrid and again started dealing with the bureaucracy. The shooting permit was refused several times. After many problems, permission was given and the film was begun on October 29th in Toledo. Exterior shooting lasted there until the end of November. Everything went perfectly: the producers had assembled one of the best teams of professionals that can be found in Spain. Buñuel had insisted that it should be a 100 per cent Spanish work. The foreign co-producers were allowed to bring in only one minor technician each and the two foreign stars; the leading role is actually that of Don Lope, played by a Spaniard . . . if not that of the film director himself. The Spanish essayist and playwright Max Aub has written that the star of the movie is not la Deneuve but the artificial leg! Buñuel was born in a village where the Virgin worked a miracle in the sixteenth century: she replaced the leg of a man who had lost it months before, joining it back onto the very same stump. It is no wonder that this erotic childhood memory has led Buñuel to film the inserting and removing of legs so frequently, both in *The criminal life of Archibaldo de la Cruz* (1955) and in *Tristana*.

Catherine Deneuve was an admirably disciplined actress and satisfied Buñuel even more than in *Belle de Jour* (1966). Fernando Rey is an old friend of his, and only the young beginner who plays the deaf and dumb Saturno had to be rehearsed and allowed many takes. The weather was perfect: sunny and clear, very cold, although less so than it appears in the film: the snow scenes were, of course, faked. Buñuel likes freezing weather and felt quite at ease. Not so much the tender Catherine, who caught some chills, yet hardly interrupted her work. Buñuel works quickly and efficiently. He knows exactly how he wants the scene to be framed and taken. Possibly he has many hesitations, but somehow he solves them during the preceding night. . . . What an admirable professional he is! He demands more freedom from the producers than any other film director, but afterwards he is most loyal to them, making economies every minute, never wasting time. Often, a working day was reduced to three hours. The rest of it was left to general preparations and to something that Buñuel, a good surrealist, considers essential to human dignity: leisure.

On December 1st, interior shooting started at the new Siena Studios, 20 miles away from Madrid; it lasted until Christmas. The work had been relaxed. There had been many visitors in Toledo, including François Truffaut and Jean-Claude Carrière. Some relations appeared as extras; Luis' sister, Conchita, and two friends played the mourning ladies. Atmosphere and art direction were excellent and Buñuel added a few last-minute touches, such as a passing soldier, a seller of lottery tickets or old-fashioned cigarette lighters, things he had seen there in the Twenties.

The film was edited in January and the sound track was completed in Paris in February. The world première took place in Madrid and Rome at the end of March. It was an unqualified success.

The final film

At a first private showing we were all surprised: Buñuel had shot the film without any plastic adornments, going straight to essentials. Whilst editing he had frequently cut some frames at the beginning and end of almost every shot, even the shortest ones. Thus the spectator is plunged into the centre of each piece of action, without the connections of the traditional grammar of film construction. This is what Luis Buñuel has always tended to do. The French New Wave learned this editing technique from him. But here, its use was so drastic that it affected the whole film.

Just because Buñuel has avoided all artistic temptations during the course of his career, he arrives here at a personal aesthetic. Well, what does that matter, one may ask, since in Buñuel the content is always the important thing? But in a real work of art, form and content are one. Buñuel's method destroys the possibility of a relaxed contemplation of the film;

he has eliminated the 'spectacle' concept, thus distancing the audience from the plot, in a similar way to Brecht's technique of alienation. A melodrama is reduced to a formula: as in a chemical laboratory or a mathematical operation, we take given data (the political, social, economic, religious traditions and habits of a given people in a given media) and the result is inevitably the one we obtain. By transposing the situation to 1928 and stating that it is still valid today, Buñuel shows that the facts described are not anecdotic, but historical constants. It is not surprising that the French film critics, with their mania for hanging tags, classed *Tristana* as a Marxist film. Buñuel, with his telegraphic treatment, has transformed a dramatic analysis into a synthesis, a historico-political tragedy, showing that whatever changes were necessary for the liberation of Tristana, Don Lope and their whole society are still to be made.

Every good film must be seen several times so as not to miss the illuminating details. *Tristana* is one of them. And then there are a great number of elements which guide the imagination further and reveal implications inherent in the plot. But when reading this text, I advise the contrary. Do not abuse the imagination! Do not visualise more than is written, because the script of *Tristana* is already *Tristana*. A rare quality indeed, and the highest praise that can be made of a film script.

April 1971

(J. Francisco Aranda has been the Spanish correspondent for 'Sight and Sound' since 1955. His book, 'Buñuel, a critical biography', won the award for the best cinema book in Spain, 1970, and will soon be published in England.)

CREDITS:

Scenario by	Luis Buñuel in collaboration with Julio Alejandro
Based on the novel by	Benito Perez Galdos
Directed by	Luis Buñuel
Produced by	Robert Dorfmann
Production companies	Epoca Film — Talia Film (Madrid) Selenia Cinematografica (Rome) Les Films Corona (Paris)
Director of photography	Jose F. Aguayo
Chief cameraman	Jose F. Aguayo junior
Assistant cameramen	Alberto Panaigua Jose A. Noya
Assistants to the director	Jose Puyel Pierre Lary
Art director	Enrique Alarcon
Production manager	Juan Estelrich
Edited by	Pedro del Rey
Sound engineers	Jose Nogueira Dino Fronzetti
Wardrobe	Rosa Garcia
Make-up	Vicente Martinez
Catherine Deneuve's hair-styles by	Julian Ruiz
Exterior locations	Toledo
Interior scenes	Siena Studios
Shooting begun	October 1969 in Toledo
Process	Eastmancolor
Length	8731 feet
Running time	98 minutes*
First shown	Madrid and Rome, 1970

---

* This figure is for the version released in England. The French-dubbed version was 105 minutes.

CAST:

Tristana	Catherine Deneuve
Don Lope	Fernando Rey
Horacio	Franco Nero
Saturna	Lola Gaos
Saturno	Jesus Fernandez
Don Cosme	Antonio Casas
Headmaster	Sergio Mendizabal
Bellringer	Jose Calvo
Don Ambrosio	Vicente Soler
Dr. Miquis	Fernando Cabrian
Don Candido	Juan Jose Menendez
Citizen	Candida Losada
Girl	Maria Paz Pondal
with	Antonio Ferrandis
	Jose Maria Caffarel
	Joaquim Pamplona

TRISTANA

The credits, which are very short, come up against a very high angle long shot of a Spanish provincial town.* In the background is a church tower, its bells ringing loudly. We are in the year 1929.

The film begins on an open space just outside the town. Two women dressed in black come towards us. They are SATURNA and TRISTANA. The former is a tall, desiccated woman of about forty years of age, rather masculine in appearance and modestly dressed; she has the air of a servant. The second woman, TRISTANA, is twenty years old; she is slim and pretty, with an air of almost childish innocence; her hair-style is simple and unaffected and her clothes do not exactly flatter her — she is wearing a slightly threadbare black dress, which sits awkwardly on her graceful body, and a small black veil over her blond hair.** The two women come into the foreground, and camera pans to follow them in back view as they walk on towards a group of adolescent youths playing football.

Medium shot of the football game with the two women watching in the foreground, back to camera. The youths obviously belong to a school, since they are all wearing the same blue overalls. A teacher or supervisor is acting as referee. From time to time he waves a small white flag which he is holding in his right hand and gives an order. Camera pans across the players. There is one curious feature about this scene, which is that not a single voice is to be heard, not a single shout, and indeed the only noise is that of the players' feet scuffing the ground, or kicking the ball. The noisy enthusiasm which one would

---
* Although the name of the town is never specified in the film, it is in fact Toledo.
** The original script stated that: ' The actress who plays Tristana should not have plucked eyebrows. She is not to be made-up, except of course to the extent demanded by the colour photography.'

expect to accompany an activity of this kind is totally absent.

[Another group of pupils, as silent as their fellows, are playing at knuckle-bones. From their wordless gestures we realise that this is a school for the deaf-and-dumb.]*

Medium shot, tracking with the players. Two youths are seen fighting for possession of the ball. They are SATURNO and ANTOLIN. SATURNO is about sixteen, with a lively expression and small, intelligent eyes in a face which has not been well endowed by nature. He is ugly but attractive. ANTOLIN, who is about the same age, is less well built, but has an equally expressive face. At first, SATURNO has the ball.

High angle medium close-up of the players' feet and the ball. ANTOLIN tries to get it away from SATURNO and finally succeeds. SATURNO is furious, and trips up his school-mate. ANTOLIN falls heavily to the ground while camera tilts up to show SATURNO's face.

Medium close-up of the two women, TRISTANA and SATURNA. The latter is SATURNO's mother.

SATURNA drily: *Huh . . . it would be him!* She sighs.

Resume on the youths. ANTOLIN gets up and advances towards SATURNO with clenched fists. After a short, tense argument conducted in gestures, they come to blows. The SUPERVISOR and the HEADMASTER of the school rush forward to separate them. The HEADMASTER berates SATURNO, who watches the former's lips. And when he turns his head away so as not to ' hear ' what he is saying, the HEADMASTER takes his head in both hands and turns it to face the front again, forcing him to lip-read his lecture.

HEADMASTER: *We've had just about enough of this. The next time I'll beat your ears off . . . for all the good they are to you! . . . Come on, come on!*

SATURNO gesticulates wildly, as if trying to explain the reason for the quarrel, but the HEADMASTER holds him by the arm and leads him away, while ANTOLIN stares

---

* This scene in brackets, taken from the original script, was not shot.

after them and the others carry on with their game.
Medium shot, tracking with the HEADMASTER, as he brings SATURNO across to TRISTANA and SATURNA. The HEADMASTER shakes hands with SATURNA. SATURNO seems bowled over by TRISTANA's beauty and stands gaping at her, but the others do not notice.

SATURNA: *I always find you up to some mischief!*
HEADMASTER: *Saturno's not a bad boy. . . . A little scatter-brained, but he's bright enough. Sometimes, he has some strange ideas.*
SATURNA: *That's a chip off the old block. . . . He's just like his dead father, God rot his soul . . . if you'll pardon my saying so.*

SATURNO moves away from the group slightly, still looking at TRISTANA, and goes off. SATURNA introduces TRISTANA to the HEADMASTER.

SATURNA: *This young lady is the ward of Don Lope Garrido. She hasn't been out of the house for a fortnight, so I thought . . . I brought her here to get a breath of fresh air. . . .*

The HEADMASTER shakes TRISTANA by the hand, and she lowers her head shyly.

HEADMASTER: *Delighted to meet you, señorita.*

TRISTANA suddenly moves her head in SATURNO's direction.

TRISTANA: *Excuse me.* She goes off.

Medium close-up of TRISTANA as she beckons to SATURNO. He comes up and they stand facing one another. TRISTANA tries to 'speak' to SATURNO by means of gestures. He is astonished by her mourning clothes.

TRISTANA in a murmur: *It's Mama. . . . She died recently.*

Then, realising that he will not understand, she raises her eyes to heaven. SATURNO understands and sadly nods his head; he clasps his hands together like a laid-out corpse, then looks up to heaven also. A pause. TRISTANA opens her handbag, takes out an apple and hands it to SATURNO. Delighted, he rubs it on his coat, and immediately takes a big bite out of it. The other youths can be seen playing in the background. (Stills on page 25)

Resume on SATURNA and the HEADMASTER.

HEADMASTER: *Your son has reached the statutory age; he can't stay at this school any longer.*
SATURNA sighing: *Yes indeed! It's time he earned his living.*
>Camera tracks out in front of them as they begin to walk side by side.

HEADMASTER: *He's a gifted boy, but he's always got his head in the clouds. He's very absent-minded, very vague . . . but at any rate, if he sobers up a bit as he gets older, he could make a good craftsman.*
>TRISTANA joins them again, followed by SATURNO, still munching his apple.

SATURNA to the HEADMASTER: *Don Lope — I work for him, you know — has found him an apprenticeship.*
HEADMASTER: *Ah! A great man, Don Lope. There aren't many left like him.*

>On these words, the scene changes to the street where TRISTANA lives, near a small square. Camera tracks with DON LOPE as he crosses the square on his way to TRISTANA's. He looks a well-preserved sixty and is carefully dressed, almost with affectation, his face lightly powdered and, one may be sure, his hair dyed. He also carries a cane. He suddenly sees someone off-screen, and halts on the corner, stroking his moustache.
>Reverse angle shot of a pretty young GIRL carrying a basket covered by a white cloth as she comes up the slope towards him. DON LOPE appears, back to camera, in the foreground.

DON LOPE ogling her: *Where are you going to, my pretty maid?*
GIRL scornfully: *Off to find a boyfriend.*
DON LOPE: *Then look no further, my pet, he is found.*
>The GIRL walks on. (Still on page 26)

GIRL shrugging: *A bit old, aren't you?*
DON LOPE: *Not as old as all that. . . . There's life in the old dog yet.*
>The GIRL goes off. At that moment a LADY appears, accompanied by a boy of about ten; they are obviously figures of some standing in the town. The LADY has wit-

nessed Don Lope's exchange with the Girl and her expression is half mocking and half scornful. Don Lope's attitude changes immediately. He takes off his hat and greets the Lady with a great show of respect.

Don Lope: *Good afternoon, madam.*

Slightly surprised, she returns his greeting with a nod. Camera follows Don Lope as he goes into a house of modest appearance. Camera tilts up over the façade.

The scene changes to the living room of Tristana's apartment.* It is modestly furnished, and the furniture itself is in a lamentable state. A balcony looks out onto the street. One door opens into the corridor and a second into another room. There are cardboard boxes and packed-up belongings everywhere. The pieces of furniture are piled up one on top of the other, ready to be taken away. We have the general impression that the inhabitants of the apartment lived in a state of scarcely disguised poverty. Yet a detail here and there, amongst the furniture and the old curtains, leads one to suppose that in the past the family may have been quite well off.

[Saturna and Tristana are packing up the bed linen. The former looks at a sheet which is almost worn through and puts it in a box. She does the same with another sheet.

Saturna: *This one is very worn already. It would do nicely for my brother. . . . Will you let me have it, Miss Tristana?*

Tristana nods. Saturna rolls up the sheet and puts it in a parcel of things which she has no doubt put aside for herself.]**

The actual sequence starts on a medium shot of the closed door of the living room. Saturna, who is near by, picks up a fox-terrier which has been sleeping on an armchair. The door opens to reveal Don Lope, who comes in and surveys the room. Camera follows him as he moves towards Tristana, who is standing near a window. She has a cloth tied over her head to protect her hair from the dust.

---

* The original script gives a general description of the décor of the room, which is quoted here, though as will be seen from the passage which follows it, this décor is only gradually revealed.
** This scene from the original script was not shot.

Don Lope *looking round the room*: *You're not going to take all that, are you?*
Tristana *humbly*: *As you wish.*
Don Lope walks round the room.
Don Lope: *All this old rubbish can be sold off. I don't want it in my house . . . there's enough there already! . . .* He calls: *Saturna!*

Don Lope's piercing glance seems to pick out what is worth keeping. Saturna comes up to him.
Don Lope: *Call a rag-and-bone man and sell him all this stuff . . . except for the linen which is usable. And don't haggle, I know what you're like. Take what he offers you.*
Saturna: *Yes, sir.*

Saturna returns to her activities. Camera pans as Don Lope walks back towards Tristana, who has been listening without daring to interrupt. He realises that she may be attached to her things and says to her more gently:
Don Lope: *If there's something you're particularly fond of . . .*

She picks up a crucifix and shows it to him.
Tristana: *Yes, this figure of Christ. . . . My mother was holding it when she died.*

Don Lope takes the crucifix, examines it without interest and hands it back to her.
Don Lope: *Very well. Take it, but keep it in your room. With a bit of time I shall root out some of those superstitions your head is filled with. . . . Of course, if you want to take anything else . . .*
Tristana: *No.* She puts the crucifix away.
Don Lope: *Right then, with that and the piano, I think that's all.*
Tristana: *The piano! . . . That was sold months ago.*

Camera accompanies Don Lope and Tristana as they go into the latter's room. Don Lope seems somewhat put out and is anxious to verify what Tristana has just said. She points to some music books lying on a desk.
Tristana: *There's just the music left. I would like to take that. One never knows, perhaps one day . . .*
Don Lope: *Very well. . . . Ah . . .*

He looks at the empty space where the piano should be and his eye falls on a framed portrait of the dead woman, on which has been placed a small black ribbon.

DON LOPE: *My child, your mother was a good woman. There was none better — nor was there ever a head with less brains in it than hers.*

He picks up the framed portrait and looks at it pityingly.

DON LOPE: *Once your father was both rich and well, but that was too long ago to do you any good. Even when you were very little, the debts were already beginning to take everything.*

He hands her the portrait, caresses her cheek and goes off. Camera holds on her for a second.

Medium shot of the living room. Camera pans as DON LOPE comes in through the door and goes across to SATURNA, who is standing in the middle of the room, making up a bundle of things with a saucepan in her hand.

DON LOPE: *Leave that saucepan! . . . I told you I didn't want to take any rubbish.*

SATURNA: *You don't know a thing about cooking, and I could make use of this. . . .*

DON LOPE looks at her severely and SATURNA reluctantly puts the saucepan down in a corner. DON LOPE addresses himself more gently to his ward, who has just come into the room.

DON LOPE: *And you must get ready, we're leaving. . . .*

TRISTANA looks around her.

TRISTANA: *Already?*

DON LOPE: *Yes.*

SATURNA: *You know what she came out with just now? She said she wanted to stay and live here. . . .*

DON LOPE looks at TRISTANA, who lowers her eyes. She removes the cloth from her head and puts a shawl around her shoulders, avoiding DON LOPE's eyes.

DON LOPE: *Listen to me, my child. . . . I can't maintain two households and you cannot live alone. Therefore . . .*

TRISTANA picks up her mourning veil from the table and gets ready to go out. DON LOPE looks at her, full of pity, with a degree of paternal affection.

DON LOPE: *On her deathbed, your mother entrusted you to me. Where else would you be better off than under my care, and who would dare to harm you, knowing that you live with me?* He picks up his hat. *Come on, now . . . we're going.*

They go towards the door and DON LOPE goes out first. TRISTANA turns in the doorway and looks around sadly. [As soon as they are out of the room, SATURNA returns to the corner where she put the saucepan; she picks it up again and, with an air of decision, puts it on the bundle of things to be taken away.]*

Medium shot from the street, looking towards the entrance of the apartment building. DON LOPE appears and descends the few steps into the street. TRISTANA follows him. Camera moves with them along the street. Suddenly cries are heard off and they stop on the street corner.

VOICE off: *Stop thief! . . . Stop thief! . . . Stop him!*

An urchin hurtles into view with a woman's handbag in his hand. He passes in front of DON LOPE and TRISTANA and makes off up an alleyway, camera panning after him. (Still on page 26)

Medium shot: a man runs into view from the same street as the urchin and rushes up to DON LOPE. He turns over his coat-lapel to show that he is a policeman.

POLICEMAN: *Did you see an urchin run past?*

DON LOPE coldly: *Was he carrying a handbag?*

POLICEMAN: *Yes!*

DON LOPE raises his cane and indicates a street, which is not the one taken by the urchin.

DON LOPE: *He went that way.*

Camera pans with the plain-clothes POLICEMAN as he glances up the alleyway, then joins a colleague. He points in the direction indicated by DON LOPE and the two men immediately rush off away from camera, on the wrong track.

Resume on DON LOPE in medium close-up; he watches

---

* This section was cut in the editing.

them go with satisfaction. TRISTANA looks at him in amazement.

DON LOPE: *Come on. . . .*

TRISTANA in bewilderment: *But . . . he went down that street there. Why did you say that . . .*

DON LOPE: *Because he was the weak one, and he had to be protected.*

They walk on up the street, camera tracking after them.

DON LOPE: *The police represent the principle of strength and a man such as I always defends the weaker party, whoever it may be and in whatever situation he may find himself. Don't forget that, Tristanita . . . don't forget it. . . .*

TRISTANA seems disconcerted by her guardian's reasoning, but she says nothing. They go away into the distance.

The scene changes to DON LOPE's apartment at night. DON LOPE's household consists of a study, a dining room, a small living room, a kitchen, a small bathroom, three bedrooms, only two of which will play a part in the film, and a corridor.

The sequence opens with a general shot of the living room. It contains a table of almost ministerial proportions, somewhat dilapidated, and a few pieces of carved furniture in dark wood, stately rather than comfortable in appearance; one fine-looking picture and several empty spaces where paintings must have hung previously; two ornamental arrangements of fencing weapons — foils, rapiers and sabres — above a large fireplace; also some fencing masks and gloves. SATURNA is engaged in cleaning the glass front of a large clock. Beside her is a small bowl, a sponge, and a dishcloth. Camera pans across to TRISTANA seated at the big table. She is polishing some objects, and now applies herself to a silver frame which contains the portrait of a very beautiful woman, dressed in the fashions of thirty years before. While she polishes the frame, we can read in her eyes the admiration which the portrait inspires in her.

TRISTANA sighing: *Isn't she beautiful . . . and so elegant!*

SATURNA comes up and stands behind TRISTANA.

SATURNA: *She was a very grand lady, married to a marquis. Don Lope got up to his usual tricks and . . . oh, what a to-do!*
TRISTANA surprised: *What did he do?*
SATURNA: *Oh dear me! . . . He challenged the husband to a duel. There was a terrific scandal, it even got into the papers.* . . . Sighing: *There's not a better man anywhere, but the moment he sees a skirt, out comes the cloven hoof!*

The bell rings at the front door. SATURNA puts down her bowl and hurries off.

High angle medium close-up as TRISTANA picks up the cloth she has been polishing with. In doing so, she knocks the bottle of cleaning liquid onto the ground. A small puddle of the liquid spreads across the floor. TRISTANA immediately kneels down to clean it up. Camera tilts up to show SATURNA in the background, opening the front door. DON LOPE comes in, takes off his hat and coat and hands them to SATURNA . . . then makes a face as he sees TRISTANA, who is still kneeling down cleaning the floor. He comes forward.

DON LOPE brusquely: *Get up, Tristana! You haven't come into this household to be a maid. You're the mistress here, and Saturna is here to serve you. . . . Saturna, clean that up!*

TRISTANA has got up obediently and SATURNA now goes to finish cleaning up the mess. Camera pans with DON LOPE as he goes towards the fireplace and drops into an armchair. He relaxes and stretches his legs. TRISTANA stands close to him.

DON LOPE: *I'm tired, my dear. I've done a lot of walking. My feet are done for.*
TRISTANA: *Would you like me to bring you your slippers?*
DON LOPE: *Yes, thank you . . . you are an angel.*

TRISTANA goes out, followed by SATURNA. DON LOPE gives a sigh and starts to undo his shoes. [He stops for a moment and looks with disgust at the portrait which TRISTANA has left on the table.]* TRISTANA comes back and, kneeling down in front of DON LOPE, finishes taking off his shoes for him and puts on his feet a pair of worn

---

* This section from the original script was not shot.

24

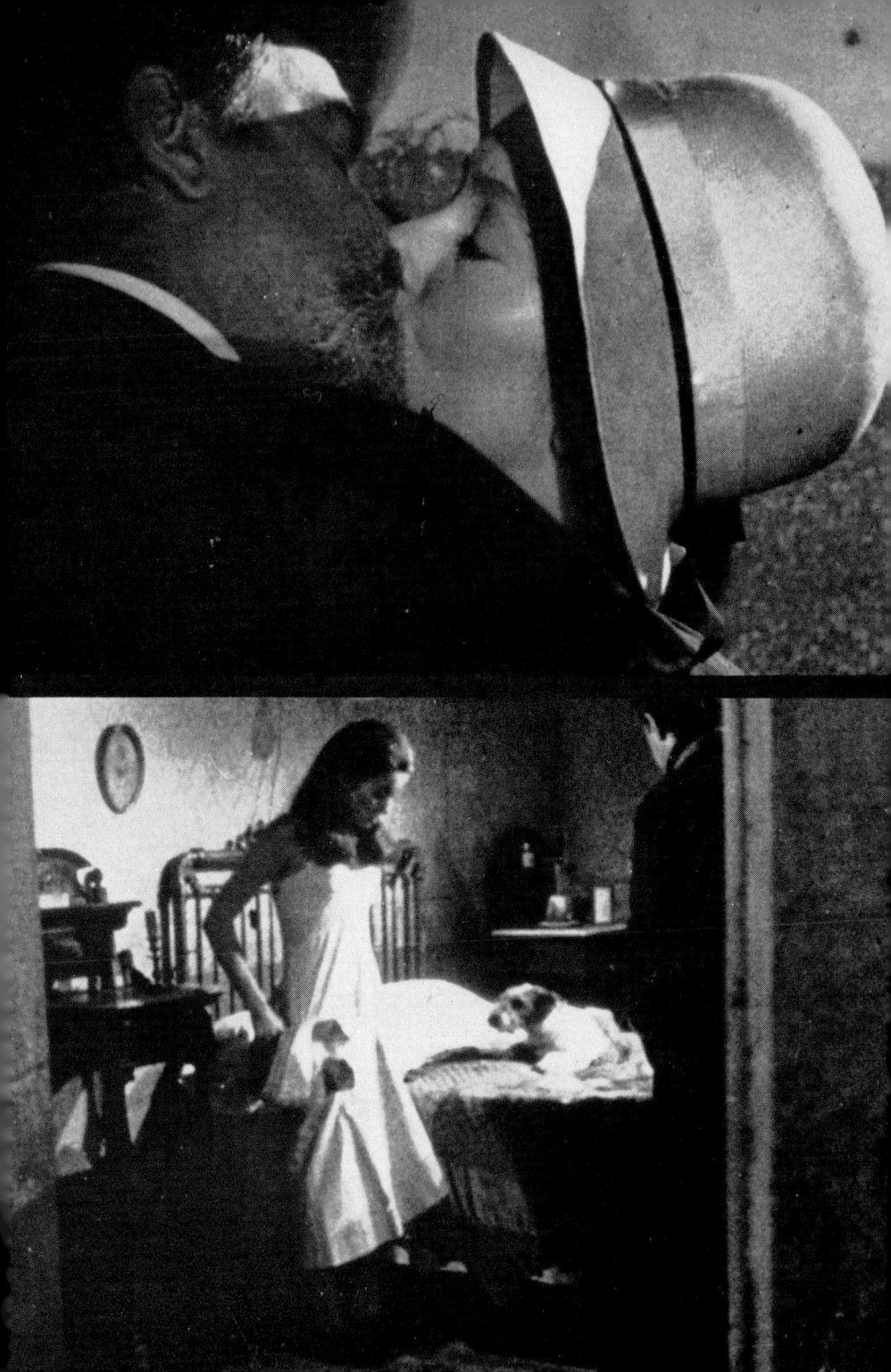

leather slippers.

Don Lope: *I hate keeping you shut up at home all the time, but what can I do? . . . I can hardly take you to the café or for a walk with my chums. And all this mourning business complicates things too. . . . The day you decide to forget about it, I'll take you to the theatre. It's up to you. . . .*

She gets up and stands in front of him, the shoes in her hand.

Don Lope: *Thank you, Tristanita. Shall I tell you something? . . . You're a darling little girl. I only want you to love me as a father.*

Still holding the shoes in her hand, Tristana gives an affectionate smile and deposits a kiss on Don Lope's forehead.

Tristana: *You're very good to me. . . .*

At that moment there is a ring at the door.

Don Lope: *Damn, I'd forgotten. . . . Someone's coming to see me.*

We see Saturna going along the corridor in the background to open the door. Don Lope gets up and motions Tristana to leave the room.

Tristana: *You're going to receive them in slippers?*

Don Lope: *Don't worry, they're friends of mine. . . .*

Tristana goes out through the door which opens into Don Lope's bedroom and shuts it behind her, while Don Lope goes towards the door leading into the corridor.

Medium close-up of Don Lope as his two friends come in through the door of the living room. One of them has white hair and they are both very elegantly dressed.

Don Lope: *Come in!*

Don Cosme: *Good evening, Lope.*

Don Lope: *Good evening.*

Don Lope shuts the door and comes back towards the two men, who are standing with their coats still on.

Don Lope: *Please sit down.*

Don Cosme: *We won't keep you for a moment.*

The two men remain standing in the middle of the room. During the discussion, Don Lope goes to the fireplace and takes down a sword, then walks round the room, playing

with the weapon.
DON LOPE: *Well now, gentlemen, when is the duel to take place?*
DON COSTE: *Tomorrow.*
DON LOPE: *At what time?*
DON COSTE: *Seven o'clock.*

> DON COSTE has sat down; DON LOPE continues to walk round the room with the foil in his hand, camera following his movements.

DON LOPE: *Where abouts?*
DON COSTE: *In the little wood.*
DON LOPE: *How will I get there?*
DON COSME: *We'll come and pick you up.*
DON LOPE: *What are the weapons?*
DON COSTE: *Sabres.*
DON LOPE: *What are the conditions of the encounter?*

> DON LOPE moves back towards DON COSTE, camera panning with him.

DON COSTE: *The party whom we represent and his opponent are both agreed that the duel should stop when the first blood is drawn.*
DON LOPE furious: *It's not possible! . . . At first blood?*

> He goes back to the fireplace.

DON COSTE: *Yes.*
DON LOPE: *And you think that I'm prepared to act as umpire for a farce like that?* He bangs his sword on the ground. *I have no taste for circus performances. I do not believe that honour can be washed away with a scratch.* Camera tracks in on him. *I'll leave the young whipper-snappers to settle with their own consciences. . . . Gentlemen, in future you need not ask me to adjudicate such worthless affairs of honour.*

> He turns and hangs his foil up above the mantelpiece.*
> [Exterior shot: a small wood in the daytime. The duel takes place. The two adversaries are standing face to face,

---

* This section was modified during the shooting. In the film, the scene in DON LOPE's living room is as described above. In the original script, however, the living room scene was shorter and DON LOPE's disparaging comments about the duellists occurred at the end of the following duel scene, which was not shot. In spite of the repetition involved, we have, for the sake of clarity, quoted the duel scene in its entirety.

accompanied by their seconds who, in accordance with the conventions, are standing a few yards away from the duellists. In the background we can see the DOCTOR laying out his instruments and, further away, the cars which have brought the combatants and those with them. DON LOPE, acting as umpire, presents the two adversaries with the swords which he is holding cradled in his arm, their hilts outwards. They take the weapons and place themselves in position for the fight. DON LOPE takes another sword with which to intervene in the duel when it is demanded by the rules.

DON LOPE solemnly: *Gentlemen! On guard! ... Proceed, gentlemen! ...*

The duel begins. The two combatants are more or less equally matched in their mediocrity.

Shot of one of the duellists in the heat of the fight.

A similar shot of the other duellist.

Another shot of the two of them lunging at each other furiously.

DON LOPE follows the course of the duel closely. One of the combatants touches the other on the arm. DON LOPE places his sword between those of the combatants.

DON LOPE: *Halt!*

The two men immediately stop fighting. The DOCTOR runs up and with the umpire's agreement examines the arm and shoulder of the wounded man.

DOCTOR: *Laceration of the epidermis. The wound is bleeding. ...*

DON LOPE looks at the combatants and says in a loud, clear voice:

DON LOPE: *First blood ... do you declare yourselves satisfied, or do you wish to continue? ...*

The victor looks at his seconds for a moment, then at the wounded man, and abruptly moves towards him with his hand outstretched. The wounded man hesitates for a moment, then reluctantly shakes the proffered hand.

DON LOPE can hardly believe his eyes. His eyes are shining with anger, but he finally manages to say in a choked voice:

Don Lope: *Reconciliation. Honour is satisfied.*
From a distance, we then see all the members of the party gravely or joyfully shaking each other by the hand, while Don Lope walks away with a scornful air. One of the seconds whom we saw at Don Lope's apartment comes towards him.

Second: *Don Lope, won't you come and take breakfast with us? . . . This calls for a celebration. . . .*
Don Lope looks at him scornfully.

Don Lope: *Go and celebrate by yourselves since you like circus performances. I do not believe that honour can be washed away with a scratch. I'll leave the young whipper-snappers to settle with their own consciences. . . .*
He goes up to a tree, still holding his sword.

Don Lope: *I'm giving my notice. In future, you need not ask me to adjudicate such worthless affairs of honour.*
He thrusts his sword into a crack in the tree and breaks it with a sudden movement. He throws the hilt end to the ground and moves away with dignity towards one of the cars.]

[Exterior shot of the cathedral tower, daytime. Camera tilts up over the façade of the tower.]*
Medium shot of Tristana in back view on the gallery at the top of the tower. On either side of her, the two deaf-and-dumb youths, Saturno and Antolin, are looking down at the roofs of the town. Saturno has placed his hand on Tristana's back and tries to caress her. Tristana, who has been pointing out various places in the town with her finger, turns round abruptly, outraged.
(Still on page 27)

Tristana indignantly: *Oh! . . Oh! . . . Idiot!*
She slaps Saturno and turns towards Antolin, who sneers and gives her a punch. The two youths laugh and start to rush away down the steps from the gallery. Tristana follows, singing out:

Tristana: *The last one there's a cissy!*

---

* This shot appeared in the French version of the film but was not seen in the English print screened.

They run off, laughing and shouting, camera panning with them as they go down the stairs and up some others. Medium close-up of the three of them as they rush through a door which leads into the BELLRINGER'S room. The scene changes to the interior of the BELLRINGER'S room. We see the doorway in low angle medium shot as the three enter. TRISTANA hesitates.

BELLRINGER off at first: *Come in, señorita, come in. I know Saturno's mother works where you live.*

While he speaks, camera pans with TRISTANA as she moves across to where the BELLRINGER is standing. He is frying small pieces of bread in a frying pan over a small stove. ANTOLIN, who is his son, is 'talking' in sign language to his friend SATURNO in the background; the youths look happy and gay.

[TRISTANA turns towards ANTOLIN, a little surprised to see him on such good terms with SATURNO, and says:

TRISTANA pronouncing clearly: *Oh, so you've made it up . . . just as well. But watch out for him. He's a good-for-nothing.* (She means SATURNO.)

The deaf-mutes explain to her by means of gestures that even if, from time to time, they come to blows, that doesn't stop them being good friends. The BELLRINGER decides that the bread is ready.]*

TRISTANA: *Mmmm, that smells good!*

BELLRINGER to TRISTANA: *I've made some fried bread. Would you like to try some, señorita?*

TRISTANA bends over the stove to look at the contents of the pan.

TRISTANA: *I'm very fond of fried bread. I wouldn't mind a bit.*

She takes off her gloves, while the BELLRINGER indicates the modest sideboard.

BELLRINGER: *Take a plate.*

TRISTANA goes to the sideboard and takes a plate. Camera

---

* This sequence was modified during the shooting. In the original script, it is only TRISTANA and SATURNO who go up the tower. As they are going up a staircase, SATURNO goes behind her and tries to look up her skirt. Offended, TRISTANA suggests the race to the BELLRINGER's room.

pans as she goes and sits down at the table in the middle of the room. She is followed by the BELLRINGER, carrying the pan, who serves her immediately. In the background, in one corner of the room, the two youths continue their conversation in sign language.

BELLRINGER modestly: *It's a poor man's dish, of course, but I'm sure you will excuse us. If I had known you were coming, I would have put in a bit of sausage. . . . Would you like a fried egg?*

TRISTANA: *No, thank you. . . . I'm expected home for lunch.*

The BELLRINGER passes behind TRISTANA, sits down opposite her and helps himself to some fried bread. (Still on page 27)

TRISTANA: *You know, I've never been up the tower before. As Saturno is a friend of your son's and today is a holiday, I asked him to come.* Camera tracks in on the two of them. *I've always wanted to go up there to see the bells, and to hear them ring.*

In the background the two deaf-mutes ' talk ', holding up a bird cage.

BELLRINGER: *Those boys wouldn't even hear the cannon of '42.*

Both he and TRISTANA eat heartily, and for a moment they concentrate entirely on their plates.

TRISTANA: *What a beautiful view you have from here. . . . You are lucky to be able to look at that every day. You must feel very important up here. It's as if you owned the whole world!*

BELLRINGER off-handedly: *Oh . . . well . . . when one never sees anything else one ends up by not noticing it. And as for being important . . . even a cat's better off. . . . In the old days, yes . . . we were important then, but now . . .*

TRISTANA: *And why not now?*

BELLRINGER: *Well, you see, señorita, in the days when there was lots of religion, the bells told people about things and they obeyed them. There was the bell for when a man was dying, then the death-knell, the tocsin, the peal for the gloria, the mass and all the bells summoning the people to prayer . . . and the people heard them . . . and they went to visit the dying man, and bury the dead . . .*

Close-up of the BELLRINGER.
BELLRINGER: *... and to fetch their guns when we sounded the alarm. Now times have changed.* Camera pans to TRISTANA; he continues off. *Everybody's so busy chasing after money. They don't listen. They even complain to the town council about our ringing for mass, because they say — can you believe it — that we wake them up.... A little more fried bread, señorita?*

Camera pans across the table, showing the two empty plates and the frying pan. There is still a little fried bread left in the pan. TRISTANA holds out her plate.

TRISTANA: *Yes, I'd love some.*

He serves her. She eats.

[BELLRINGER off: *If you want to hear the big bell, it will be ringing fairly soon.*

TRISTANA: *Oh, yes! ... I really would like that!*

Medium shot of the room.

BELLRINGER: *Nothing simpler!*

The two deaf-mutes move towards the door. TRISTANA gets up, smiles and hurries out.]*

Interior shot of the staircase leading to the belfry. The door of the BELLRINGER'S room opens as TRISTANA and the two youths come out. Camera pans with TRISTANA as she goes and looks through the keyhole of another door. Taking advantage of this, SATURNO goes up and taps her on the back, urging her to climb the staircase. Laughing, she begins to do so, and he passes in front of her.

TRISTANA: *Go on, up you go.*

He does not hear her, but goes on up all the same. She follows him.

Resume on them in high angle medium shot at the top of a staircase in the tower. TRISTANA bends down to look through a window. Meanwhile ANTOLIN, who is behind her, lifts up TRISTANA'S dress. She whips round angrily and slaps him.

TRISTANA: *Stop fooling!*

Camera pans as they go on up the stairs.

---

* This section did not appear in the version screened.

Medium close-up as they go on up another staircase, camera panning after them. They reach a bend in the staircase. A bell begins to ring off.

High angle medium close-up as they come up the staircase, TRISTANA last.

High angle medium shot as they come up the steps into the belfry, which is flooded in sunlight, and start to walk about amongst the bells. As the bell continues to ring, the noise of the mechanism can be heard. Camera follows TRISTANA as she walks in wonderment amongst the bells. SATURNO touches her on the arm and gestures out of the window. (Still on page 28)

[ANTOLIN, the BELLRINGER's son, takes TRISTANA by the arm and stands her under the big bell just as it starts to ring. TRISTANA is overcome by the noise and vibration and shrinks back, stopping up her ears, and goes and leans against the wall. The youths laugh like madmen, then suddenly become serious, as if they were trying to hear the noise. SATURNO lays his finger on the wall. Apparently feeling the vibration, he points it out to his friend, who nods affirmatively, having tried the same thing several times before.]*

Shot of the bell ringing. It stops.

Medium shot: TRISTANA looks under the biggest bell. She tries to push the clapper. (Still on page 28) Suddenly she freezes and an expression of extreme astonishment comes over her face, followed by one of extreme fear. Zoom in on her face.

Reverse shot of what she is looking at: instead of the clapper, she sees DON LOPE's head swinging under the bell. His eyes are half open. We hear TRISTANA cry out.

TRISTANA off: *Saturna! . . . Saturna! . . . Saturna!*

The scene changes to TRISTANA's bedroom at night. Medium shot of TRISTANA starting up in bed, her mouth still open from her cry. Her face is panic-stricken. The door opens, and SATURNA comes in and turns on the light.

---

* Cut from the versions seen.

She is wearing a nightgown with a small shawl around her shoulders. She runs towards the bed and takes TRISTANA in her arms, trying to calm her. (Still on page 29)

SATURNA: *What is it, Miss Tristana? . . . What was that cry for?*

TRISTANA: *A dream, Saturna . . . I had a horrible dream. It was terrifying . . . the bell! . . .*

SATURNA: *There, there, calm down, now . . . it's all over.*

Long shot of the corridor. DON LOPE, dressed in a long night-shirt flapping round his spindly legs, comes out of his room pulling on his dressing gown.

DON LOPE in alarm: *What's the matter, my child? Are you ill?*

Resume on TRISTANA'S bedroom. DON LOPE comes in and camera pans as he goes over to TRISTANA'S bed.

SATURNA: *She had a nightmare, sir . . . the poor little thing!*

DON LOPE: *Make her one of your mixtures . . . a lime tea . . . anything . . . get a move on!*

SATURNA hurries out. DON LOPE sits on the edge of the bed and strokes TRISTANA'S hair.

DON LOPE: *Come, now . . . come, now! Calm down. . . . It's all over. . . .* Smiling: *You screamed as if you'd seen the devil himself.* Laughing: *I remember, when you were little, you used to scream in exactly the same way whenever you saw me. . . .*

The two of them look at each other. For the first time DON LOPE notices that TRISTANA'S nightgown is undone at the front, partly revealing her breasts.

TRISTANA: *It's over now. . . . I think you can go.*

DON LOPE: *It's good to have dreams, even if they're frightening.*

TRISTANA scratches her breast.

DON LOPE: *The dead don't dream.*

He pulls her nightgown together. At the same moment, the expression on his face changes, and his look seems to become clouded over. (Still on page 29)

DON LOPE: *Well, good night, my child.*

He kisses her and goes off; camera holds on TRISTANA as

she watches him go.*

The scene changes to a square in the town. It is market day. Amongst the stalls, Don Lope can be seen, coming towards camera. He is wearing a black bowler hat and an elegant black cape with a red lining. He has his cane in his hand. He stops for a moment near two soldiers, to light a cigar.

High angle general shot of the interior of a large provincial café. There are numerous men seated at small tables, smoking and talking. Camera tracks sideways across the customers to show Don Lope as he enters in the background. He makes his way among the tables, greeting and being greeted by all the habitués of the place. He always replies in a friendly but slightly distant manner. It would seem that he is generally held in some respect by the café's clientèle. During Don Lope's progress across the café, various voices are heard calling out to him.

Voices: *Good afternoon! . . . How are you? . . . What's new? . . .*

At the back of the café are his friends — about six men whose ages vary between fifty and sixty. They are all talking animatedly, but the conversation ceases the moment they see Don Lope approaching. He takes off his hat and cape and hands them to a Waiter. Don Cosme gets up to make room for him on the bench seat. Don Lope sits down and Cosme sits beside him.

Don Lope: *Good afternoon, gentlemen.* He turns towards the Waiter, who is waiting politely. *The usual, Antulio.*

Friends: *Good afternoon, good afternoon . . .*

'The usual' is a white coffee, which the Waiter will bring in due course. Don Lope looks at his friends and says, sarcastically:

Don Lope: *What's the matter, has the cat got your tongues? Why did you all stop talking when you saw me? Carry on . . . carry on with all the unpleasant things you were saying about me.*

---

* End of reel one, 600 metres.

They all look at each other, rather embarrassed. One or two of them smile maliciously.

Medium close-up of the two men seated on either side of DON LOPE. One of them, DON ZENON, begins to protest.

DON ZENON: *What an idea, Don Lope, no one would dare to . . .*

DON LOPE: *Well, I can assure you that when you're not with us, Don Zenon, we certainly dare to make fun of you. . . .*

DON COSME, who is seated on the other side of DON LOPE, bursts out laughing. DON LOPE turns towards him and says:

DON LOPE: *And we talk about you, too, when you're not here. So I don't see why you should wish to spare me. . . .*

Camera pans to show the opposite side of the table.

DON ANTONIO: *You say it as if not talking about you in one way or another showed a lack of consideration. . . .*

Pan back to COSME, with another man in back view in the foreground.

DON COSME: *To tell the truth, we were beginning to run out of subjects. We've talked about everything but you. . . .*

DON LOPE: *Thanks.*

Camera pans and tracks in on COMMANDANT PELAEZ, who is seated at the opposite end of the table.

COMMANDANT PELAEZ: *But we've also been commenting on the fact that you've given up umpiring duels. . . . Is it true or only a rumour?*

Close-up of DON LOPE.

DON LOPE: *It's true, Commandant — true that there are no more men like there were in my day . . .* He looks at the others and, sweeping his eyes across the group, corrects himself: *. . . in our day.*

Slight track back to show his neighbour.

DON ZENON: *At least there's one thing on which today and yesterday are in agreement — the taste for a fine wench. . . .*

DON LOPE: *Agreed, although nowadays there's so much effeminacy.*

Pan across to the COMMANDANT.

COMMANDANT PELAEZ: *It's always intrigued me, Don Lope, that you, who are such a stickler for principles in matters of honour, are so broad-minded when it comes to the sins of love.* . . .

> One or two of the men clear their throats, perhaps considering the question to be improper.
>
> Medium close-up of DON LOPE. He takes his cigar out of his mouth and gestures benevolently.

DON LOPE: *There's nothing to worry about, the question is quite justified. For my part, as far as love affairs and women are concerned, I consider that sin just doesn't come into it.* . . .

> Camera tracks back to show the whole group from above.

VOICES: *Really, Don Lope.* . . . *If only it were true.* . . . *That would be all very nice.* . . . *Now there's a theory for you!* . . .

DON ZENON in shocked tones: *What about the Ten Commandments?*

DON LOPE: *I respect them all, except for those concerning the fair sex, because I'm certain that they were added to the real divine commandments by Moses, for political reasons which don't concern me.* . . .

> Two or three men burst out laughing.

DON ZENON: *You've got to watch out for Don Lope!* . . .

DON COSME: *So you propose that wherever we find one of the fairer sex* . . .

> He makes an expressive gesture, which provokes general laughter. The WAITER comes partly into view and, as DON LOPE speaks, he puts down the cup of coffee.

DON LOPE: *Not so fast, my friend . . . not so fast! There are always distinctions to be made. Wherever we find one of the fairer sex, if she is consenting — and it is up to us to make her so — then let the encounter be a pleasant one . . . but with two obvious exceptions* . . . Camera tracks in on him; he sugars his coffee as he speaks . . . *the wife of one's friend and that strange flower, so rare these days, which is born of perfect innocence.*

> As he finishes off we cut to a medium close-up of TRISTANA. She is sitting at the table in DON LOPE'S living room, looking at her books of music and making the motions of playing the piano on the table. It is even-

ing. In the corridor outside, we hear SATURNA banging on a door.

SATURNA shouting, off: *Come out of there, you little scamp! . . . Saturno! Saturno! . . . Come out of there, once and for all!*

TRISTANA abandons her music reading and gets up; camera follows her as she goes over to the door.

High angle medium close-up of TRISTANA'S dog sniffing at the lavatory door in the corridor.

TRISTANA off: *What's the use of calling, if he can't hear you?*
SATURNA off: *He hears when he wants to.*

Medium shot of SATURNA standing in front of the lavatory door, banging on it. TRISTANA stands behind her.

SATURNA: *He can't hear me? I'll stop this craze for shutting himself away if I have to beat it out of him. He's been in there for an hour.*

She turns towards the door again and shakes it, trying to open it. The dog whines.

SATURNA: *Open up, or I'll kill you!*

TRISTANA pushes her aside and, taking hold of the door knob, turns it gently several times. Immediately we hear the bolt being drawn and SATURNO comes out. He looks uneasily at his mother. The latter doesn't waste any time and immediately cuffs him. SATURNO tries to protect himself with his hand, but his mother attacks him again.

TRISTANA: *Come, now, there's no need to beat him. . . .* She tries to put herself between them.

SATURNA: *I know what I'm doing and so does he. . . .*

She pushes him and shakes him like a fruit tree. He tries to justify himself in sign language.

SATURNA: *Go on, be off with you. Your uncle doesn't like you arriving late.* To TRISTANA: *And he's quite right. After he's been working all day on his scaffolding he likes to get to bed early. . . . He's kind enough to tolerate this wretch in his house as it is. . . .*

She pushes SATURNO towards the front door of the apartment. TRISTANA follows.

Medium shot: the front door opens and DON LOPE comes in, apparently in a bad mood. SATURNO and his mother appear.

Don Lope to Saturno: *What are you doing here?*

Embarrassed, Saturno takes off his beret to greet Don Lope and tries to explain with gestures.

Don Lope roughly: *Never mind . . . never mind. . . . Yes, get out!*

Saturno goes out. Don Lope takes off his hat and cape, which he hands to Saturna, then he goes towards Tristana and kisses her on the forehead.

Don Lope: *Dinner!*

Finally he goes into the dining room, followed by Saturna. Camera holds on Tristana, who moves off on the opposite side of the corridor.

Inside the dining room, Don Lope sits down at the table, which is laid for dinner. He takes a newspaper out of his pocket, unfolds it and begins to read. [Meanwhile we can still hear the voice of Saturna.

Saturna off: *One of these days they're going to sack him from that workshop. The owner says he's picking up all kinds of bad habits.*]*

Tristana hurries in with Don Lope's slippers. Camera tilts down as she comes and takes off his shoes, as if it were a customary ritual. Don Lope, who is absorbed in his reading, does not even notice. (Still on page 30)

Don Lope reading: *The original sin of the First Spanish Republic, was to try and cure the gangrene of the institutions by speeches, and speeches only.* He sneers: *What rubbish!*

As he reads aloud, in a scornful tone, Tristana puts on his slippers. Tilt up as she goes off, taking the shoes with her.

High angle shot of the table. Saturna is partly visible as she puts down a dish, then puts a boiled egg on a plate in front of Don Lope. Camera tracks out to show the three of them: Don Lope is seated facing Tristana; Saturna is standing waiting for orders. Don Lope puts down the newspaper and is just about to break his egg when he sees that Tristana has not got one and is reduced to a helping

---

* Not heard in the versions screened.

of vegetables.

DON LOPE: *I see we are having the everlasting boiled egg again . . . as we did yesterday.* To TRISTANA: *What about you . . . aren't you having an egg?*

TRISTANA: *I'm not hungry.*

DON LOPE shrugs his shoulders, but SATURNA intervenes.

SATURNA: *It's not true, sir. The fact is there was only one and we gave it to you.*

DON LOPE pushes the egg-cup across to TRISTANA. (Still on page 30)

DON LOPE: *Here. Eat it.*

She tries to refuse, but he insists.

TRISTANA: *No thank you.*

DON LOPE: *Eat it, I said.*

He gives her the egg. Bowing her head, TRISTANA begins to break the shell with a knife, while DON LOPE turns to SATURNA, who is bringing the bread basket.

DON LOPE: *And you — why haven't you brought anything else to eat?*

SATURNA: *And what would I buy it with? . . . You don't want me to get things on credit.*

DON LOPE: *My income just isn't enough to make ends meet. . . . Well, we'll have to find a remedy for that.* He begins to help himself to spinach.

Medium close-up of him facing camera.

DON LOPE: *Ah, filthy lucre! Whether we like it or not, my child, we are all its slaves. And it only ceases to be filthy when we give it to someone who has the misfortune to need it, whoever that may be.*

He suddenly breaks off. Camera tracks out to include all three of them.

SATURNA: *If you'll allow me to say so, sir, all that about whoever it may be — well, it depends.*

DON LOPE: *This spinach is revolting!*

SATURNA: *When you have neither money nor appetite, you're always in a bad temper, and when you're in a bad temper you're not satisfied with anything. . . .*

DON LOPE: *Give me the wine!*

She does so. DON LOPE eats in silence. He is surprised to

see tears on TRISTANA's cheeks.

DON LOPE: *What's the matter?*

TRISTANA does not reply. DON LOPE turns towards SATURNA.

DON LOPE: *What's the matter with her?*

Medium close-up of TRISTANA with her eyes lowered. SATURNA comes up to her.

SATURNA: *What do you think's the matter with her? She's thinking of her mother ... or else she's feeling stifled. She's been shut up in here for weeks now.*

DON LOPE off: *Doesn't she go to mass?*

Pan to follow SATURNA as she comes back towards DON LOPE, who pours himself some wine.

SATURNA: *What kind of fun is that for her? She goes, anyway, probably not so much from devotion as to get out of the house. ... You ought to let me go out with her now and then, so that we can get a bit of sun.*

DON LOPE: *If you want an honest woman, break her leg and keep her at home.* To TRISTANA: *Have you got anything to say?*

Medium close-up of TRISTANA, her eyes full of tears. She shakes her head.

TRISTANA: *Me? No, sir.*

Medium close-up of DON LOPE and TRISTANA sitting face to face. She is in the foreground, three-quarters back to camera.

DON LOPE: *You always seem to be wearing the same dress. Haven't you got any others to wear?*

TRISTANA: *No, sir.*

DON LOPE: *Well, we must put an end to that! ... You're a sorry sight as you are now. ... And as from tomorrow, no more mourning! I'm going to get you some new clothes.*

TRISTANA begins to cut a piece of bread.

High angle shot of the boiled egg. TRISTANA's hand dips a finger of bread in the yolk. Camera tilts up as she pops the bread in her mouth.

DON LOPE off: *All this mourning business is sheer barbarism. It's like painting your face or tattooing your body.*

The scene changes to Don Lope's study. It is daytime. High angle shot of a whole service of silver plate on the table. There is also a silver ewer from the dining room. Camera tilts up slightly to show an Antique Dealer who is assessing the items. Don Lope stands beside him and Don Cosme a little way away.

Antique Dealer: *This is Meneses silver. That's worthless. This is genuine silver. They're good pieces. There's no doubt about that . . . but they're difficult to sell here.*

Don Lope interrupts him brusquely.

Don Lope: *How much?*

Antique Dealer after a pause: *Well, now . . . I'd give two thousand pesetas for that.*

Don Lope makes a grimace and goes and takes a picture down from the wall. He hands it to the Antique Dealer.

Antique Dealer looking at a piece of paper: *You say it's genuine and the documentation seems to confirm it . . . but an unsigned picture! . . .*

He looks at Don Lope and the latter shoots a furious glance at him. Somewhat disconcerted, the Dealer says:

Antique Dealer: *If it were anyone else I would give three thousand pesetas, but . . .*

Don Lope's attitude is distinctly scornful.

Don Lope: *None of your buts. . . . I don't ask for favours, nor shall I accept them. Give me five thousand pesetas.*

Don Cosme exclaims indignantly and walks off into the living room.

Antique Dealer: *But, Don Lope, in view of the respect I have for you . . .*

Don Lope with a bitter smile: *Respect is not something to be haggled with. Give me the five thousand pesetas including the dish.*

Camera tracks in on them slightly.

Antique Dealer: *Give me a few moments to make an inventory of what I'm going to take.*

Don Lope: *Take your time.*

He moves away. The Antique Dealer, papers in hand, starts to list the objects.

Medium shot of Don Cosme pacing around the living

room. DON LOPE comes in and stands facing him while SATURNA appears through the doorway in the background.

DON COSME: *You could have got much more out of him. It's a crime to sell those pieces for that amount.*

DON LOPE: *I hate haggling.*

SATURNA, a little embarrassed, makes so bold as to approach DON LOPE.

SATURNA: *Do think again, sir.*

DON LOPE brutally: *Get back to your kitchen, you.*

She goes out.

DON COSME: *If I had known a little earlier, perhaps I could have . . .*

DON LOPE: *I don't do business with my friends.*

DON COSME: *So much the worse for you!*

Pan as he follows DON LOPE across the room.

DON LOPE less harshly: *I can't stand the commercial mentality, Cosme. From that cheapjack in there to the big industrialists who deal in millions, they're all the same — vampires. . . . Let's go and see what the rascal's up to.*

Camera pans as they walk towards the study. DON COSME tries to hold DON LOPE back by the arm.

DON COSME: *Listen, Lope, we might still . . .*

DON LOPE shaking himself free: *Leave me alone.*

DON COSME: *Come now, I'm sure he could be persuaded to give you a better price.*

*[The scene changes to a cubicle in a dress shop, in the daytime. From DON LOPE's face pronouncing his last words, we move to that of TRISTANA as she raises her arms to put on a new dress, helped by a SALESWOMAN. The garment includes a kind of bolero which hides the shape of her breasts. TRISTANA looks at herself in the mirror with childish curiosity, while the SALESWOMAN goes towards the door and opens it.

SALESWOMAN: *You can come in now, sir.*

DON LOPE enters. He looks at TRISTANA affectionately while she turns right round, blushing slightly, so that he

---

* The following scene was cut in the shooting.

can see how the dress looks on her.
SALESWOMAN: *What do you think of it?*
DON LOPE: *Well, I can hardly congratulate you. It makes her chest look as flat as a board. Pardon my saying so, but she looks more like a man seen from behind.*

The SALESWOMAN takes off the bolero. The dress is in fact fairly low cut and shows off TRISTANA's shape perfectly. DON LOPE appears satisfied.

DON LOPE: *Now I see the point — you cover it up at first . . . so you can uncover it later.*
SALESWOMAN: *You'll take it then?*
DON LOPE: *Yes . . . and also put in the two plainer little dresses that we chose just now.*

The SALESWOMAN goes out. TRISTANA is still inspecting herself happily in the mirror. DON LOPE comes and stands beside her. He puts his arm round her waist and stands up as straight as he can.

TRISTANA: *I feel so strange. . . . It doesn't look like me at all.*
DON LOPE looking at himself with her: *You're very pretty. . . . Though I say it myself . . . I think we make a fine couple.*

TRISTANA smiles at her reflection. Without taking his eyes from the mirror, DON LOPE draws TRISTANA against him and puts his face close to hers, still with his arm round her waist. Their cheeks almost touch and DON LOPE's lips graze TRISTANA's small, delicate ear. She jumps slightly, and looks at him in astonishment. He laughs and pats her reassuringly on the back.

DON LOPE: *Come come, now . . . don't be silly!*]

Exterior shot of a large renaissance courtyard, daytime. A line of little girls are seen in medium shot, walking two by two away from camera, led by a nun. As they go off, DON LOPE and TRISTANA appear, the latter looking very smart. Arm in arm, they walk along an arched colonnade and pass two children, each pulling a toy engine on a string.

Another similar shot. Behind them come their parents. The mother is pushing a pram, while the husband is keeping an eye on one of the children who has got left behind. TRISTANA and DON LOPE stop. DON LOPE turns round, and casts a mocking glance after the couple in their Sunday best. The family goes off.

DON LOPE: *Look at that charming little couple. Can't you just smell the sickening odour of marital bliss?*

TRISTANA looks at him in astonishment.

TRISTANA: *I don't understand . . .*

DON LOPE: *Look at their attitude of bovine resignation, look how bored they are. Love is finished for them. Dear little Tristana, don't ever get married.*

They continue to walk.

Medium close-up, camera tracking out in front of them.

TRISTANA: *One can be free without being dishonourable, can't one?*

DON LOPE: *Exactly. Passion should be free. It's a matter of natural law. No chains, no signatures, no benedictions.*

Camera pans, losing him, as TRISTANA looks up.

Low angle shot of the pillars of the colonnade as seen by TRISTANA, camera tilting up and down over them.

TRISTANA off: *Which of these pillars do you prefer?*

DON LOPE off: *Now it's me who doesn't understand.*

Medium shot of the two of them. DON LOPE comes towards her. TRISTANA is looking at the pillars intently.

TRISTANA: *I said, which of these pillars do you prefer?*

DON LOPE: *None . . . or any of them . . . they are all the same.*

TRISTANA: *No two pillars are ever the same. If you look carefully you can always see the difference. I always choose between things — between two grapes or two bread rolls or two snowflakes . . . because there's always a little something which makes me like one of them more.*

Camera follows TRISTANA as she circles round a pillar. DON LOPE comes up behind her as she puts her arm round it.

TRISTANA: *This is the one I prefer!*

DON LOPE: *Well, you'd better pick it up and take it home then . . . and let's change the subject.*

They move away, backs to camera.

The scene moves to the interior of a church, daytime.

High angle medium close-up of a head sculpted in marble on a tomb.

Close-up of Tristana in profile as she leans over it, her face very close to the figure's mouth. (Still on page 31)

Another shot of the figure's head. Tristana is still leaning over the figure, almost lying on it.

Medium shot of the tomb. As Tristana gets down from it, Don Lope comes up to her. They are alone in the church. Camera tracks in on the two of them. (Still on page 31)

Don Lope: *What were you doing up there?*

Tristana: *I was thinking that you need another pair of slippers.* She smiles.

Don Lope: *What's that? . . . Come along. . . . Let's go.*
They go off.

We see them again in the cloister outside the church. Don Lope has put his hat on. Suddenly he stops and gazes at Tristana with some emotion.

Don Lope holding her by the arm: *There are times when I think that you like me . . . and others when I think that you don't . . . sometimes I even have the impression that I repel you a little.*

Tristana astonished at this idea: *Repel me? . . . No, what an idea! On the contrary.*

Don Lope: *Then . . . you don't find me unattractive?*

Tristana: *No.*

Don Lope: *In that case . . . perhaps you even love me a little?*

Tristana sincerely: *Yes.*

He casts a furtive glance around him and draws her into a corner. Camera tracks in on them. At that moment his eyes are shining and full of intensity. Although he is three times as old as the girl, the couple they make is neither grotesque nor laughable. The man's arrogance temporarily compensates for the wide difference in their ages.

Don Lope with great emotion: *Kiss me!*

Close-up of the two of them, favouring Tristana. Don Lope is three-quarters back to camera. She obediently kisses him on the cheek.

Don Lope *impatiently*: *No, not like that.*
And, clasping her to his chest, he kisses her on the lips. (Still on page 32) Tristana is astonished, but does nothing to avoid the kiss. After a few seconds, Don Lope draws away from her. Perhaps from emotion or surprise, without really realising what she is doing, Tristana bursts into nervous laughter. Then she pulls herself together and lowers her eyes.

The scene changes to the kitchen of Don Lope's apartment. It is evening. Saturna is seen in medium close-up in the centre of the kitchen, grinding coffee in a small coffee-mill. Footsteps are heard in the corridor outside.
Don Lope *off*: *Saturna!*
Saturna: *Yes, sir?*
Saturna goes to turn on another light in the room while Don Lope appears in the doorway, wearing a dressing gown.
Don Lope: *Weren't you going to see your brother?*
Saturna: *Yes, sir. I've finished grinding the coffee. I'm going straight away.*
Don Lope: *Hurry up then.*
Saturna: *Yes, sir.*
Don Lope disappears and Saturna takes a shawl which is hanging on a nail and throws it around her shoulders. She turns out the light and goes out of the kitchen.
Shot of the corridor. Saturna makes her way towards the front door at the end. She passes Don Lope, with his pipe in his mouth, carrying the dog in his arms.
Saturna: *Are you sure you don't need me any more?*
Don Lope: *Yes, yes. Quite sure, quite sure. Take your time.*
Saturna: *Yes, sir. Until later then, sir.*
She opens the door and goes out. Don Lope puts the dog down on the floor and goes off, adjusting his dressing gown.*
In the living room, camera pans to show Tristana stand-

---

* The original script describes the dressing gown as 'a threadbare garment which is, however, kept clean by being frequently washed by Saturna'.

ing at the table in the centre of the room, ironing. She is wearing one of the little zephyr dresses which DON LOPE gave to her. Camera tracks back to show the rest of the room. Beside TRISTANA is a pile of ironed linen. DON LOPE, who has just come in, clears his throat off-screen. Camera pans to include him as he watches her working for a moment. He gives a curious smile. His manner has changed: his movements and gestures are full of assurance, of the certainty born of dominating a submissive and obedient prey. Slowly, he comes up to TRISTANA, who jumps and turns round. She stands motionless, as if in anticipation of something which disturbs her considerably.

DON LOPE: *Have you finished?*
TRISTANA: *I've still got one . . .*
DON LOPE: *Leave it. . . .*

Still with the same curious gleam in his eye, DON LOPE puts his arms round TRISTANA and feasts his eyes on her for a moment.

TRISTANA: *What if she comes back?*
DON LOPE: *She won't come back before dinner time. And anyway, it's time she got used to it.*

Holding TRISTANA round the waist, DON LOPE leads her towards the door. In the doorway, he kisses her on the mouth. Her lack of resistance seems to indicate that this is not the first time this scene has taken place. The door closes on the two of them.

Outside in the corridor, camera pans and tracks along the wall to the open door of TRISTANA'S bedroom. TRISTANA is standing beside the bed, taking off her dress in front of DON LOPE. The dog is lying on the bed. (Still on page 32) When TRISTANA is in her underwear, DON LOPE picks up the dog and carries it out into the corridor, coming towards camera.

DON LOPE to the dog: *What do you think you're doing here? . . . Be off with you now.*

Meanwhile TRISTANA has sat down on the bed and begun to take off her stockings. DON LOPE closes the door in the foreground.

THE YEAR 1931*

Exterior shot of a street in the daytime. A group of demonstrating strikers come running towards us. Some bend down to pick up a stone or a brick, others raise their fists. They are pursued by policemen carrying sabres.

Long shot of a square. Riot police on horseback are lined up ready to charge. The strikers are heard shouting angrily off-screen.

High angle long shot of the strikers, shouting and hurling insults. Camera pans across to the mounted policemen. One of their leaders gives a signal to the bugler, who immediately sounds the charge. (Still on page 65)

Shot of a street corner. (Still on page 65) Some workers run past DON LOPE'S house, pursued by soldiers on foot with drawn sabres. Pan as the group of fugitives and their pursuers disappear, then camera zooms in on DON LOPE'S front door. One of the demonstrators has managed to hide in the doorway; it is SATURNO. He looks from right to left, then slips rapidly into the house.

Medium shot, tilting with SATURNO as he climbs the steps two at a time and goes out of sight.

Inside DON LOPE'S apartment, SATURNA, who is carrying a warming pan, hears a ring at the front door. Camera pans as she goes to open it, and SATURNO comes in.

SATURNA furious: *What have you been up to this time, you little hooligan? I've already told you not to go sticking your nose into those demonstrations. They're nothing to do with you.*

SATURNO tries to explain with gestures that he is a man and everything concerns him as much as anyone else.

SATURNA shrugging: *Come and say good morning to Don Lope and Miss Tristana, then be off with you.*

She pushes him along the corridor.

Shot of DON LOPE'S bedroom. SATURNA comes in carrying the warming pan, pushing her son in front of her. DON LOPE is sitting in the centre of the room in a monastic-

---

* Note in the original script.

looking armchair. He is wearing a dressing gown, with a rather grubby night-cap on his head. His legs are covered with a tartan rug. He blows his nose, then expectorates.

DON LOPE to SATURNO: *And what mischief have you been up to, eh? Sit down . . . sit down.* He gestures to the other side of the room.

Camera pans with SATURNO as he comes across the room, passing TRISTANA, who is standing at the foot of the bed, apparently preparing some medicine. He shoots an admiring glance at her. Meanwhile, SATURNA lifts the bed covers and inserts the warming pan into the bed, moving it to and fro. Two years have passed since DON LOPE took TRISTANA into his home. She has become more self-confident and assured. DON LOPE has aged considerably. We notice that the dye has partly grown out of his hair and his wrinkles have deepened. He no longer bothers to wear make-up in the intimacy of his home.

DON LOPE irritably: *I can't stand this any longer. . . . Tomorrow I'm going out.*

TRISTANA very coldly: *I don't think you will be better by tomorrow. . . . There's no point in getting upset.*

Camera follows TRISTANA as she goes over to DON LOPE, holding a medicine bottle and a spoon.

DON LOPE: *I hate inactivity, and above all I hate you seeing me in this ridiculous state.*

TRISTANA: *You were bound to fall ill some day . . . especially at your age!*

On hearing these words, DON LOPE starts, and throws an angry glance at TRISTANA. She looks at him imperturbably.

DON LOPE: *I don't see any connection between my age and having a cold. . . . I'd like to see one of those young puppies who think they're so hearty with a cold like this one!*

He has been moving his legs restlessly and the blanket has slipped down slightly. TRISTANA leans forward to pull it up again. DON LOPE stops her and does it himself.

DON LOPE: *Leave the rug alone. I'm quite capable of doing it myself.*

At that moment, he is shaken by a fit of coughing. TRISTANA starts to pour him out a spoonful of cough-mixture, but he refuses to take it.

Don Lope: *Stop mollycoddling me all the time! . . . Leave me alone!*

Without losing her composure, Tristana moves back slightly.

Tristana: *As you wish.*

High angle medium close-up of Don Lope, with Tristana back to camera in the foreground. He has stopped coughing and his breathing becomes a little calmer. He looks affectionately at his ward.

Don Lope: *As I wish and as you wish! I'm not trying to impose my will on you. That's why we're so happy together, because neither you nor I have lost our sense of freedom.*

Tristana holds out the spoonful of cough-mixture again and this time he swallows it. A pause.

Don Lope: *At this very moment, if you wanted to, you would only have to tell me that you'd had enough of me — you could leave and I wouldn't say a thing.*

Tristana wearily: *If I left, you would catch me before I got to the end of the street.*

As she speaks, she goes and puts the medicine bottle back on the table. He bursts out laughing and, as Saturna removes the warming pan from the bed in the background, he says in amused tones:

Don Lope: *That's quite possible!*

Saturna coming up behind him: *There you are, sir. The bed's warm, now.*

Tristana helps Don Lope to get up and takes off his dressing gown for him, revealing the long white combinations which he is wearing underneath. She goes and hangs up the dressing gown, then comes back towards Don Lope, who goes towards his bed.

Don Lope: *It is you who must decide the limits to be attached to your freedom, Tristana. But bear in mind my dignity, and the affection I have for you.*

Pan with Saturna, who goes towards the door.

Resume on Don Lope, seen from above, as he gets into bed. Saturno is seated near the bed, in the background. Don Lope coughs; Tristana comes over to him immediately and ties a woolly muffler round his neck. He takes her hand and kisses it. (Stills on page 66)

Don Lope: *You are so good to me, dear child. How can I help adoring you?*

Tristana snatches her hand away from him.

Tristana curtly: *Let me go.*

But Don Lope tries to take her hand again to kiss it. We hear Saturna's voice from the doorway.

Saturna off: *Shall I serve your meal, Miss Tristana?*

Don Lope to Tristana: *Yes, yes . . . off you go.*

Camera pans with Tristana as she goes out, followed by Saturna. Before she goes, the latter turns to Don Lope, who is now off-screen.

Saturna: *Afterwards I'll bring you your broth.* She shuts the door.

Resume on Don Lope lying in bed. He coughs.

Inside the kitchen, Saturna goes towards Tristana, who is seated alone at the table. She holds out an extremely frugal dish of food.

Saturna: *They're very tasty, Miss Tristana.* She serves Tristana. *The master's so fond of you, it really does one good to see it.*

Tristana: *If only he were a little less fond of me!*

Saturna: *Poor man!*

Resume on Don Lope's bedroom, where he is seen from above, lying in bed. He is dozing lightly, comfortably propped on his pillows. Then he opens his eyes and, raising himself slightly, gives an exclamation of surprise.

Don Lope: *Are you still here?*

Camera tracks out to include Saturno, who replies with a vague gesture and comes towards Don Lope.

Don Lope pronouncing his words as clearly as possible: *What's going on out there? . . . Are they having a rough time?*

He points to the window; Saturno looks towards it, understands, and replies in sign language, indicating the fierce struggle which is going on outside. Don Lope motions Saturno to give him a purse which is on a chest beside the bed. Saturno gives it to him. Don Lope takes out a large coin and hands it to Saturno, who takes it, tosses it in the air and smiles in thanks.

DON LOPE: *Ah, the workers, poor fellows! . . . When they're not being cuckolded they're being beaten. Work is a curse, Saturno. Down with the work one has to do to earn one's living!*

DON LOPE continues his monologue, which is incomprehensible to SATURNO. He speaks partly off, camera following SATURNO as he moves around the bed.

DON LOPE: *That kind of work does not bring us honour as they claim; it only serves to fill the bellies of the pigs who exploit us. But the work one does for pleasure or from a sense of vocation — that, man is ennobled by! Everyone should be able to work like that.* Camera tracks in on him. *Look at me — I wouldn't work even to save my life, and you see . . . I may not live well . . . but I live without working.*

Medium shot of the open door. SATURNA has been listening to this little speech, and camera now pans with her as she goes towards the bed.

SATURNA: *What kind of advice is that to give to the boy! . . . Fortunately he can't hear you; if he could . . .*

DON LOPE to SATURNO: *Off you go, now. And keep clear of the truncheons outside.*

Having understood DON LOPE's gesture, SATURNO says goodbye with a little bow, and goes out accompanied by his mother. Camera holds on DON LOPE lying in bed; it tracks in on him. He coughs.

Resume on the kitchen, where we can see TRISTANA in medium close-up, seated at the table, eating. She looks at her plate of chick-peas for a moment, then takes two of them and puts them down on the tablecloth. Track in on her face. She looks from one to the other and we realise that she is playing her favourite game of choosing between them.

High angle close-up of the two chick-peas. TRISTANA's hand hesitates over first one, then the other chick-pea. She finally takes one.

Resume on her face. She slowly munches the chick-pea with a satisfied expression.

The scene changes to the town square, with arcades round the sides, which we see in long shot. It is early afternoon and most of the townspeople are either still finishing lunch or, in many cases, taking a siesta. Camera tracks and pans to look down one of the arcades. In the background, DON COSME and DON LOPE have just come out of a restaurant and are coming towards us. Camera tracks out in front of them.

DON LOPE: *Ah! . . . That was a magnificent meal!*
DON COSME: *Yes indeed, it was extremely good.*
DON LOPE: *I've still got a pretty healthy appetite, you know.*

A FRIEND comes up to them. He shakes them by the hand.

FRIEND: *Ah, Lope, how good it is to see you.* To COSME: *Good afternoon, my dear boy.*
DON LOPE: *Good afternoon.*
FRIEND to COSME: *And how are you?*
DON COSME: *Oh, in fine fettle, thank you.*

DON LOPE motions them towards their habitual café. They go towards the door. DON LOPE stands aside to let the FRIEND go in first.

DON LOPE: *After you.*
FRIEND: *No, after you.*
DON COSME to DON LOPE: *Go on . . . you go first.* They go in.

Medium shot from the street, facing the doorway of DON LOPE's house. SATURNA comes towards us, putting a shawl round her shoulders. Camera pans with her as she goes to meet TRISTANA who is waiting for her, looking very smart. They seem undecided as to which direction to take for their walk.

SATURNA: *Where do you want to go today, then?*
TRISTANA: *I don't mind.*
SATURNA rather anxious: *One day Don Lope is going to find out about these outings.*
TRISTANA: *So what? We hardly see him from one day to the next. Anyway, I don't care if he does find out. I can't stand him any longer, Saturna.*

Camera tracks sideways with them as they walk along the street.

SATURNA still consumed by anxiety: *I'll be the one who catches it for coming with you, you wait and see.*

TRISTANA: *He's getting older and more ridiculous every day.*
They walk on in silence, away from camera.
Medium shot of a narrow street. We see them again, coming towards camera. SATURNA stops for a moment and leans against a wall to adjust her shoe.

TRISTANA: *It's some time since I mentioned the bell to you. But last night I had that nightmare again.*

SATURNA: *You do have some strange ideas!* Shrugging her shoulders and smiling: *Don Lope's head as the clapper of a bell! . . .*

TRISTANA: *If only I could run away somewhere and never have to see him again in flesh and blood.*
They continue to walk in silence.
High angle shot, tracking in front of the two women, as they come to an intersection. TRISTANA stops and takes SATURNA by the arm, bringing her to a halt also.

TRISTANA: *Wait a second.*

SATURNA: *What is it?*
TRISTANA points to something and SATURNA looks in the direction she indicates.
Reverse shot of what the two women are looking at. On the other side of the intersection are two almost identical alleys, leading off in opposite directions. Camera is looking up one of them at first, then pans to show the other.

TRISTANA off: *You see that street, and that one. Which one do you like best?*
SATURNA doesn't understand.

SATURNA off: *Whichever you like . . . I've no idea.*

TRISTANA off: *Well, I prefer the one on the right. Come on.*
The two women come into view, moving away from camera up the second alleyway. TRISTANA is walking very quickly and SATURNA has some difficulty in keeping up with her.

SATURNA: *To tell you the truth, I preferred the other one.*

Camera cranes up as they go off into the distance.*
Medium shot of another deserted alleyway. A mangy-looking dog runs past.
VOICES off: *It's got rabies . . . kill it . . . call the police . . . watch out!*
Medium shot as the two women come down the street. Cries are heard off.
VOICE off: *It's already bitten a child. It's got rabies!*
High angle reverse shot of the same street. TRISTANA and SATURNA appear, seen from behind. People are milling about in the background.
A WOMAN: *The dog's over there.*
ANOTHER WOMAN: *It's gone into a house.*
TRISTANA and SATURNA look at one another rather anxiously. People run past in the background.
SATURNA: *Shall we go and watch, Miss Tristana?*
TRISTANA: *You go if you want to. I'm not very fond of dogs, especially when they're mad.*
SATURNA goes towards a couple of women, who are chatting about it in the background. Camera pans with TRISTANA, who notices a large doorway which is half open: she goes over to it and looks in.
Medium shot: camera moves with TRISTANA as she goes in through the doorway and pauses, looking into the courtyard.
Medium close-up as TRISTANA moves forward and finds herself in a kind of half-ruined cloister belonging to an old disused convent.
Reverse shot of what she sees: the cloister is overgrown with weeds, hedge-mustard and ivy, which have climbed around the broken columns, sprouted between dislodged blocks of stone, or formed drooping cascades from the cornices.** Almost in the centre of the cloister are two men, standing beside a small donkey. One of the men is dressed in Catalan regional costume. The other, dressed

---
* End of the second reel, 600 metres.
** Contrary to this description taken from Buñuel's original script, the cloister appears to be in the process of renovation, and noises of building operations can be heard as the scene proceeds.

as an artist, recalls the stereotyped image of the painter. He is so busy adjusting the pose of his model, who is holding up a flask of wine, that he does not notice either TRISTANA's presence or the sounds coming from the street. Satisfied with his model, the painter clambers over some blocks of masonry and sits down in front of his easel. Camera pans with him.

Resume on TRISTANA watching with curiosity. Camera pans as she comes up to the painter and stands over him.

TRISTANA embarrassed: *There's a mad dog in the street, so I . . .*

The painter, whose name is HORACIO, says without looking at her:

HORACIO: *Make yourself at home.*

Looking up, he gives a little ironic smile.

HORACIO: *Take a seat if you feel like it.*

Medium close-up of HORACIO painting. TRISTANA leans towards the canvas. (Still on page 67)

TRISTANA: *He's a Catalan, isn't he?*

HORACIO: *Yes. I got him to come from Barcelona.*

TRISTANA: *Ah, yes.*

They look at each other. The noises in the street get louder.

Medium shot of the dog at the meeting point of two alleys.

Shot of another street corner. A POLICEMAN, revolver in hand, passes two women — one of whom is SATURNA — and goes up to a group of men. One of them points to an alleyway out of shot.

MAN: *It's over there.*

POLICEMAN: *Thanks.*

He runs off in the direction the man has indicated.

Resume on the cloister. Camera moves in a travelling crane shot across the galleries above the cloister, finally holding on a high angle shot of the courtyard below. The Catalan and his donkey are still posing while TRISTANA and HORACIO stand deep in conversation. Two gunshots are heard. (Still on page 67)

Resume on the street where SATURNA is standing with the

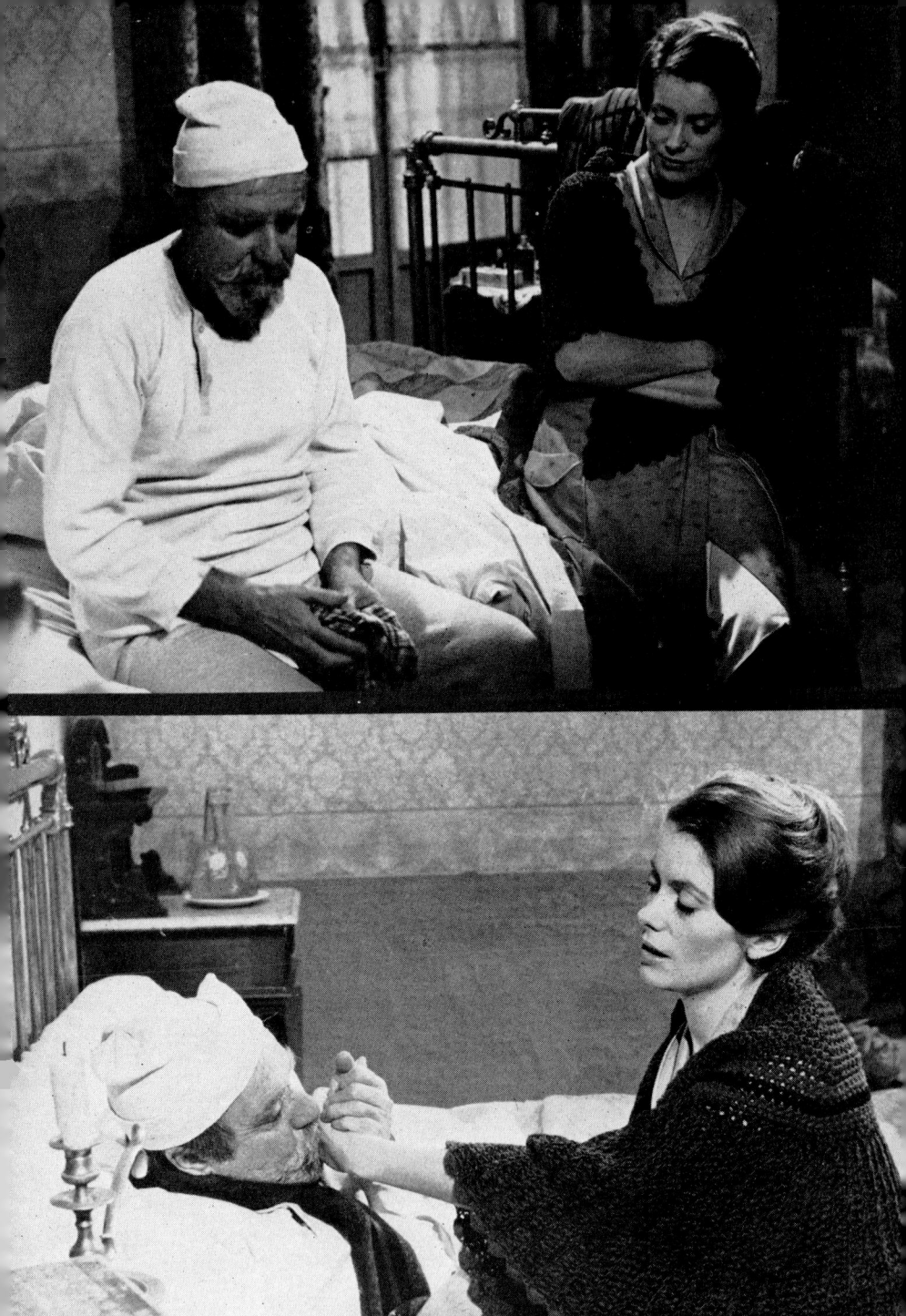

other onlookers. The POLICEMAN comes into frame and addresses the bystanders.

POLICEMAN: *Well, that one won't be biting anybody else, anyway.*

A WOMAN: *It's lucky you came by.*

POLICEMAN putting away his revolver: *I could have had him with the first shot . . . but I was in the wrong position. I was afraid the bullet would ricochet. Well, I must be off. . . .* He salutes them. *Goodbye.*

VARIOUS VOICES: *Goodbye.*

Medium shot, panning with SATURNA as she enters the cloister. She is very surprised to see TRISTANA talking to a man in the background. She stops. TRISTANA and HORACIO have not noticed her presence.

HORACIO: *But look, what have you got to lose? . . .* Insistently: *All I want to do is paint your portrait. There's nothing wrong in that. . . . It won't take long.*

TRISTANA, who has just noticed SATURNA, blushes as though she has done something she shouldn't have, and comes towards her.

TRISTANA to the painter: *No . . . No . . .*

She reaches SATURNA, then turns towards the painter again.

HORACIO: *I'm counting on you. . . .*

They go out. Camera holds on HORACIO, who watches them go. The encounter has made a great impression on him.

Medium shot of TRISTANA in the street. Very nervous, still blushing and deeply troubled by her unexpected encounter with the painter, she walks along quickly, holding SATURNA's arm. They stop.

TRISTANA: *Oh! . . . Saturna . . . how terrible! . . . What will he think of me? . . .*

They walk on again towards camera.

TRISTANA: *Without knowing what I was doing, I said yes to everything. . . . I couldn't take my eyes from his. . . . He must have thought I was mad . . . or else that I'm a fool, and he'd be quite right to think so! . . . I even told him where I lived. . . . He insisted on seeing me again, and I said he could. I'm so ashamed! . . .*

Pan as they hurry off down the street, away from camera.
TRISTANA: *Don't scold me, Saturna. If I think it's all right, I shan't regret it. . . . My God, what happens if Lope finds out. . . .*
    TRISTANA continues to speak, but we can no longer hear what she is saying as she and SATURNA move away into the distance, towards the end of the street.

    The scene changes to DON LOPE's bathroom, where we see DON LOPE in his shirt sleeves. (Still on page 68) He takes a small jar out of a cupboard. His moustache, which he has probably been dyeing, is protected by a band, which he now removes before powdering his face very carefully. When he has finished making himself up, he puts away his cosmetics and takes down his tie from a hook on the back of the door.
    Medium shot of TRISTANA's bedroom. SATURNA is putting clean sheets on the bed.
DON LOPE off: *Saturna! . . . Saturna!*
SATURNA: *Yes, sir?*
    She does not stop but continues with her work, and shortly afterwards DON LOPE appears.
DON LOPE: *Didn't you hear me? Here. . . . Iron this tie for me.*
    He looks at the bed and suddenly frowns.
DON LOPE: *Why are you making up this bed?*
SATURNA: *Miss Tristana said she wanted to sleep here . . . alone.*
    DON LOPE's face clouds over with a mixture of astonishment and annoyance.
DON LOPE: *Alone. . . . Why?*
SATURNA: *I don't know, sir.*
    DON LOPE hesitates for a moment. He is considerably affected by the news. Finally, he makes up his mind and goes out.
    [Frowning, DON LOPE walks quickly down the corridor to the living room. He draws himself up before going in.]*
    Interior shot of the living room. Link on the motion as

---
* This shot was not seen in the version screened.

Don Lope enters, buttoning up his waistcoat. Camera pans and tracks with him as he goes over to Tristana, who is sitting with a serious expression on her face, knitting. She does not raise her head when her guardian approaches. The latter looks at her angrily. On the one hand his wounded pride inclines him towards violence; on the other he realises how humiliating it would be for him to display his disappointment.

Don Lope: *Tristana!* . . .

She raises her head and looks at him steadily, almost insolently. Don Lope hesitates; he makes an effort to contain himself and ends up by improvising.

Don Lope: . . . *Get ready, we're going for a walk.*

Tristana equably: *The two of us?*

Don Lope: *And who else? It's more respectable for you to go out with me than by yourself.*

Tristana almost cynically: *You think so?*

Don Lope controlling himself with difficulty: *Get ready!*

Tristana obeys, but without hurrying. She gets up and puts down her work, then goes off to get ready. Camera holds on Don Lope, who grinds his teeth in annoyance.

The scene changes to a promenade somewhere in the town. Evening is coming on and there is a melancholy light over the scene. There is an avenue of bushy chestnut trees, and double-sided wooden benches on either side of the promenade. One or two people are out for a stroll. An old man sits quietly smoking on a bench. Two nuns pass by. As the sequence begins, camera tilts down from the trees to reveal a Pedlar carrying a small lottery wheel on his back.

Pedlar: *Try your luck!* . . . *Wafers!*

[He passes Don Lope and Tristana, who come into shot, backs to camera.

Pedlar: *Try your luck!*

He goes out of frame, while camera tracks behind Don Lope and Tristana as they walk along the avenue.]*

---

* This section was not seen in the version screened.

Medium close-up of the two of them facing camera, which tracks out in front of them as they walk. Don Lope looks very dapper, and walks with his chest thrown out slightly, swinging his cane, which he is clearly never to be seen without. Tristana is elegant and remote. Don Lope greets a passing couple. Tristana remains icily distant. They continue to walk in silence. (Still on page 68) Suddenly Tristana stops. She looks at Don Lope with a radiant smile.

Tristana: *If I suddenly started shouting for joy, would you think I was mad?*

Don Lope gives her a sour look. They walk on again, camera tracking out in front of them.

Don Lope: *You're up to no good, I can tell that. You're always going out, always away from the house. It all smells of suitors and street-corner rendezvous to me.*

Camera pans to show Tristana by herself.

Tristana: *I'm free, aren't I? If I do something wrong I have only my own conscience to answer to for it. I'm only following your advice.*

Pan to include Don Lope again.

Don Lope trying not to make his anger obvious to the passers-by: *If I catch you putting a foot wrong I shall kill you. . . . I would rather have a tragedy than be made a fool of in my old age.* They stop. *And let me tell you that you cannot keep any secrets from me. . . . With the experience I have of these things it's impossible to deceive me . . . impossible.*

By now he is almost shouting. Tristana glances around them as if ashamed that somebody may have overheard him.

Tristana: *Be quiet, Lope!*

Medium close-up of the two of them, Tristana in back view.

Don Lope: *Now you've been warned . . . and don't forget that I still have two obligations towards you.*

She looks him calmly in the eye.

Don Lope: *I am your father and your husband, and I can be one or the other as and when it suits me. . . .*

Tristana moves towards the railing at the edge of the

promenade, off-screen. Camera holds on DON LOPE as he watches her go.

Medium shot, tracking with two ladies, who approach from the opposite direction. One of them is about seventy, the other slightly younger. Their dress is slightly old-fashioned, but the older one in particular has an arrogant air and a distinctly aristocratic bearing. She is wearing mittens and leans on a rubber-tipped walking-stick. They both pass a mere yard away from DON LOPE. The one wearing mittens — DONA JOSEFINA — looks at him scornfully. She hisses at him:

DONA JOSEFINA: *Imbecile!*

DON LOPE hears her, makes a grimace and returns the insult.

DON LOPE: *Old fool!*

The two women continue on their way. After a moment's reflection, DON LOPE turns and hurries after DONA JOSEFINA. She stops and looks at him haughtily.

DON LOPE: *I need ten thousand pesetas. Lend them to me and I swear I'll give them back.*

DONA JOSEFINA: *I do not support heathens!*

DON LOPE drily: *Keep your money then, you old bigot!*

He turns and goes off. Camera holds on the two old ladies. DONA JOSEFINA tosses her head scornfully, then gives her free arm to her companion; they continue their walk, camera tracking with them.

DONA JOSEFINA: *Oh! That brother of mine, Patrito! What have I done that God should punish me so!*

DONA PATRO: *Fortunately you're the one who holds the purse-strings, my dear.*

DONA JOSEFINA: *Yes!* . . . Sighing: *But only so long as I live. Laws are made for men, my child.*

Still chattering, they walk off.

[We now see TRISTANA beside the railing, her cheek propped on her hand, smiling dreamily. She is obviously having very pleasant thoughts.]*

---

* Cut in the editing.

The scene changes to the interior of a workshop producing objects of Spanish folk-art in wrought iron. Medium shot of two workers in front of a forge, hammering a piece of red-hot iron. Camera tracks out to show other men at work. The master-craftsman is working on an object at a bench, and he looks up from time to time to keep an eye on his apprentices. Camera pans with an apprentice as he crosses the workshop, and we see TRISTANA and SATURNA as they enter. The workers watch them pass indifferently. Pan with SATURNA as she goes up to the master-craftsman, DON DIMAS. A pause, then he looks up and sees her.

SATURNA: *Good afternoon, Don Dimas.*
DIMAS: *Good afternoon. . . .* Remembering why she has come: *I asked you to come because I want you to take your son back.*
SATURNA: *Has he done something wrong?*
DIMAS: *He just won't do as he's told.*
SATURNA distressed: *You must remember his disability.*
DIMAS: *One can be deaf and dumb — and disciplined, ma'am.*
He looks round, but cannot see SATURNO.
DIMAS: *He should be over there right now. . . .* He asks a worker: *Where's the deaf-mute?*
WORKER: *Out in the yard — as usual.*

DON DIMAS goes towards the back of the workshop and SATURNA follows him, looking annoyed.

Medium shot of TRISTANA as she stands near one of the workers and watches him working.

Exterior shot of the yard. DIMAS ushers out SATURNA, then passes in front of her and points to the lavatories in the background.

DIMAS: *He's been in there for more than an hour.*
Camera tracks in on SATURNA and DIMAS as they go up to the lavatory door. SATURNA tries to open it. It is locked. She knocks on the door.
SATURNA: *Come out! Come out of there, you little wretch!*

She almost shakes the door off its hinges. It eventually opens and SATURNO comes out, buttoning up his overall and looking rather sheepish. Camera pans after him as he goes over to a tap and washes his hands. His mother goes

up to him and drags him violently towards her.
SATURNA: *Aren't you ashamed of yourself, eh? Here, everyone works, while you* . . .

SATURNO tries to explain in sign language that he was in there from necessity. His mother pushes him towards the door into the street, hitting him and berating him, illustrating her words with gestures so that he can understand what she is saying.

SATURNA: *I'm going to take you to your uncle. . . . You can work on the building site. Then you'll find out what's what.* . . .

She hits him again. He moves away.

SATURNA to DIMAS: *I must apologise, Don Dimas. . . . Thank you for everything.*

She moves towards the door, followed by DIMAS, who opens it for her.

DIMAS: *You're welcome.*

They shake hands while SATURNO goes out; then SATURNA follows, gesturing.

Reverse angle shot of the doorway seen from the street. DON DIMAS stands inside and says to TRISTANA:

DIMAS: *Goodbye, señorita.*
TRISTANA: *Goodbye.*

She comes out. He shuts the door behind her. Camera pans to look up the alleyway outside. In the background SATURNA scolds her son with words and gestures. TRISTANA stands in back view in the foreground and calls to SATURNA.

TRISTANA: *Saturna!* . . . SATURNA comes towards her. *I'm going to see him.*

SATURNA anxiously: *Don't . . . don't stay too long, Miss Tristana.*

TRISTANA remains unmoved, and replies by giving SATURNA an order.

TRISTANA: *Go home, Saturna.*
SATURNA: *You know he's taking a siesta today. What shall I tell him if he wakes up before you get back?*
TRISTANA: *Tell him what you've seen — that you left me in the street.*

TRISTANA starts to walk in the opposite direction to that

taken by SATURNO, whom his mother has sent away with a gesture. But SATURNA is reluctant to follow her son. Finally, she starts to follow her mistress.

Reverse angle shot as TRISTANA goes down the street away from camera.

TRISTANA turning round: *Go away.* . . .

She walks away, but SATURNA follows her. Camera cranes up as they go away into the distance.

Medium shot panning with the two women as they come round a street corner. SATURNA follows four or five yards behind TRISTANA, who stops in front of the door of the house where the painter lives. She turns to SATURNA.

TRISTANA: *You can wait for me here, if you insist!*

She goes into the house. SATURNA puts on her shawl and remains standing on the pavement, having obviously decided to wait.

The scene changes to the interior of HORACIO's improvised studio.* There are three doors, giving onto a kitchen, a wardrobe and a dressing room. In one corner there is a low, ramshackle bed. There are a few pictures hanging on the walls, representing different aspects and landscapes of the small provincial town. A half-finished picture stands on an easel. The occupant is evidently only a temporary resident, since apart from the general disorder which one expects to find in an artist's studio, there is something impersonal in the atmosphere, reminiscent of a hotel room. Two suitcases are piled one on top of the other on a piece of furniture. The room is lit by two windows from which there is a magnificent view over the roofs of the town. The sequence starts on a medium close-up of HORACIO, sprawled in an armchair, apparently dozing. There is a knock at the door. Camera tilts up as HORACIO gets up and joyfully goes towards the door. Far from being asleep, he is in fact wide awake, and his apparent relaxation was

---

* As in previous cases, the general description which appears in the original script is given before the start of the actual sequence. In this description, the picture on the easel was originally described as the half-finished portrait of Tristana; in the film, however, it would appear to be a landscape.

clearly only the enforced calm of a man who is eagerly awaiting someone's arrival. Camera tracks in slightly as he opens the door and TRISTANA enters.

HORACIO: *I was beginning to think you wouldn't come, my darling.*

TRISTANA taking off her gloves: *I've had so many things to do. And anyway, I can't stay for long today.*

He goes up to her, puts his arms round her and whirls her round. (Still on page 69)

HORACIO: *You'll go when I say. . . . I want to get your portrait finished.*

He kisses her on the cheek. She draws away from him and looks at him sadly.

TRISTANA: *The thing is that today he's stayed at home.*

HORACIO eagerly: *I've got some coffee ready, and I bought some of the cakes you're so fond of.*

Camera follows HORACIO as he comes back towards the table, where there is a coffee pot, a spirit stove, a packet of sugar, two cups and some small cakes.

HORACIO: *It's ridiculous that you should be so afraid of your guardian. You ought to introduce me to him some time.*

He strikes a match in order to light the stove.

TRISTANA off: *I won't have anything. Don't light it for me.*

He hesitates for a moment, then puts out the match.

HORACIO: *You haven't answered me. When are you going to introduce me to your guardian?*

Close-up of TRISTANA. She takes her courage in both hands and says:

TRISTANA: *He's not my guardian. He's something more. . . .*

A pause. She looks at him imploringly and starts to take off her hat. (Still on page 69)

Medium shot of TRISTANA, with HORACIO back to camera in the foreground.

TRISTANA: *He's my husband.*

HORACIO has difficulty in taking in this astonishing piece of news.

HORACIO: *What?*

TRISTANA begins to talk with the courage born of despair.

TRISTANA: *I've lied to you . . . and now I'm ready to tell you everything.* [*It won't do me any good . . . but I can't stop myself telling the truth.*]*

Without taking his eyes off her, HORACIO paces nervously round TRISTANA.

TRISTANA: *I'm not married to my husband . . . I mean to my guardian . . . I mean this man.* She becomes more and more emotional. *You can't imagine what I've been through. Now I've told you everything. Forgive me.*

Camera pans and tracks with her as she goes and sits down on the edge of the couch. He comes over and, as she continues to talk, he sits down beside her. (Still on page 70)

TRISTANA: *I know I'm dishonoured, but on the other hand I'm free to love you. . . .* A pause. *How does it seem to you? Can you forgive me? Tell me, how do you prefer me — as an unfaithful wife, or like this — free?*

He does not reply, but sits with his elbows on his knees, staring at the floor.

TRISTANA with tears in her eyes: *Do you still love me? Tell me!* She tries to take his hand. He pushes her away and gets up. (Still on page 70)

Medium close-up as he leaps to his feet. Camera pans with him as he walks furiously across the room. His anger is increasing every moment and as he passes his easel, he hurls it violently to the ground. TRISTANA gets up. HORACIO paces wordlessly round the room, followed by TRISTANA, who walks behind him, pleading her cause.

TRISTANA: *Say something, I beg of you! . . . You can see that the only person I've deceived is 'him', and he has no rights over me . . . but I'm free, and he quite deserves what I'm doing to him.*

HORACIO is overcome by jealousy as he listens to TRISTANA's confession.

TRISTANA: *No, I don't love him. . . . Sometimes I think I detest him for all that he's done to me, and at other times . . . I must admit . . . I used to feel affection for him, nothing more, as if I was his daughter. . . . If he had loved me like a*

---

* This piece of dialogue was not heard in the version screened.

father it would be a different story. . . . He's got a good side to him, but there are other things. . . . It makes me ashamed just to think about it. He changes his character like he changes shirts, and he shows the worst side of it when it comes to anything in skirts.

While TRISTANA has been speaking, HORACIO has picked up a large shell as he walks round the room.

Close-up of TRISTANA, looking at him with tears in her eyes.

TRISTANA: *Since I've met you, I've started to hate him . . . to hate him deeply . . . above all because you have respected me, believing me to be pure and innocent.*

Reverse angle close-up of HORACIO.

HORACIO: *The old goat!* He turns towards her and says angrily: *And what about you, how did you come to be there with him?*

He has finally broken his silence, and this gives TRISTANA renewed courage.

Resume on her.

TRISTANA: *I've already told you the story of my life. . . . When he took me in, I was an innocent girl. . . . You can imagine the rest. . . .*

Resume on HORACIO.

HORACIO: *Get out! . . . Get out!*

He picks up his easel and takes his tubes of paint. TRISTANA registers the resentment in this gesture and goes towards the table with a determined step.

High angle medium close-up of TRISTANA's hat and handbag on the table. Camera tilts up and pans with her as she takes her things and hurries towards the door in the background. HORACIO remains at his easel. TRISTANA opens the door and hesitates. A pause.

HORACIO: *Tristana!*

She stops and looks at him. He hastily puts down his tubes, strides across and shuts the door, then gazes at TRISTANA, who stands with her eyes cast down, weeping. He goes very close to her.

Medium close-up of the two of them. (Still on page 71) He lifts her chin and kisses her tenderly on the cheek.

They throw their arms round one another and kiss passionately. [Conquered by the flame she sees burning in HORACIO's eyes, TRISTANA obeys docilely when he says:
HORACIO: *Sit down!*

She sits down and he draws her to him. She gazes intensely into his eyes. He lays her down on the bed and kneels on the floor beside her. He kisses her passionately, and TRISTANA is unable to resist. In a half-smothered voice, she says:
TRISTANA: *I must go. . . . I must go.*]*

The scene changes to the interior of DON LOPE's bedroom, daytime. Medium shot of DON LOPE, who has been lying on his bed, taking his siesta. He wakes up with a start and gets out of bed. He is wearing a woollen vest and his trousers are unbuttoned, with his braces hanging down at the sides. He puts on his slippers and goes to get his shirt, which is hanging over the end of the bed. His appearance can only be described as lamentable. Seen in this state, having just woken up, he looks ten years older. He yawns.

Medium shot of the front door of the apartment from the corridor. The door opens; SATURNA looks in cautiously, then camera pans as she tiptoes towards the kitchen, leaving the door ajar for TRISTANA.

Resume on DON LOPE in the bedroom as he goes towards the door and looks out into the corridor.

Medium shot of DON LOPE in the corridor. Looking surprised, he goes towards the front door and notices in passing that TRISTANA's hat is not on the coat rack. Pan to the front door as TRISTANA enters, smiling happily and somewhat out of breath. She comes face to face with her guardian, but without turning a hair shuts the door behind her and goes to hang up her hat. On seeing his ward, DON LOPE forces himself to produce a smile. He obviously dislikes being seen in such a state; his disordered appearance makes him lose his self-confidence.

---

* Cut in the shooting.

Don Lope: *Where have you been, Tristanita — so late, and all alone too?* (Still on page 71)
Tristana very coldly: *First of all it's not very late, and secondly I am not alone.*
> Don Lope cannot help admiring Tristana. Her eyes are shining with a strange brilliance, her cheeks are flushed, and her lips are moist and very red. She looks extremely beautiful.

Don Lope full of admiration: *How pretty you look! Have you been running?*
Tristana: *Yes!*
Don Lope embarrassed by his attire: *Very well, my child . . . very well. . . . I must go and tidy up a bit. . . .*
> He takes down his hat from the rack and hands it to Tristana.

Don Lope: *My dear child, would you be so kind as to clean my hat band? I have a very important visit to make this evening.*
> She takes the hat and makes off down the corridor. Camera pans to show her from behind as she goes towards the kitchen, tossing the hat in the air. Don Lope follows her and goes back into his room, his braces trailing.
> Medium shot of the kitchen. Saturna is busy clearing away some crockery. Tristana enters and fetches a bottle of benzine to try and clean the sweat stains off the hat band, though they are almost certainly indelible. Camera pans as she goes over to the table.

Saturna in a low voice: *What luck. . . . He didn't tell you off!*
Tristana: *It wasn't for lack of wanting to, but he didn't dare. He looked frightful. He doesn't like me seeing him like that. . . . When the cock has lost his feathers, he hides.*
Saturna: *Don't be too hard on him, Miss Tristana. Poor man!*
> Camera tracks in on Tristana.

Tristana: *If he treated me differently, I would like him, you know. . . . Anyway, today I'm happy!*
> As she says these last words her eyes light up. She stands for a moment in ecstasy, staring blankly at the hat she is

holding in her hand, her mind elsewhere.

Medium close-up of DON LOPE, in the bathroom, standing in his shirt-sleeves in front of the mirror. He is dyeing his beard and moustache black with a little brush. Camera tracks in on his reflection in the mirror.

Resume on the coat rack in the corridor, where DON LOPE'S coat and cane are hanging.

DON LOPE off: *Tristana.*

Camera pans to show DON LOPE, now looking very elegant, about to go out. He takes down his coat and cane. TRISTANA approaches from the end of the corridor and hands him the hat. DON LOPE now feels much more sure of himself, and his natural arrogance has returned.

DON LOPE dignified and severe: *You and I will settle things later. We must discuss this little matter of coming and going when you please. . . . You are saved for the moment, because I'm in a hurry.* He goes towards the front door. *I have left my slippers in the bathroom. Put them back in my bedroom.*

He stops in front of the door, looks back, and then goes out with a self-important air.

[TRISTANA leans in at the bathroom door and picks up the slippers which are lying on the floor — not without a certain amount of distaste. She goes rapidly towards the kitchen.]*

Shot of the interior of the kitchen. Camera pans with SATURNA as she goes over to the sink. TRISTANA enters, carrying the slippers, and goes over to the rubbish bin. SATURNA follows her movements with a glance.

TRISTANA: *Once he's smartened up, he gets his nerve back. But it's no good, he's losing his feathers. What a disaster!*

High angle medium close-up of the rubbish bin, into which TRISTANA throws the slippers.

SATURNA off: *What if the master asks where they are?*

TRISTANA off: *Tell him to buy some more . . . or he can go barefoot . . . I don't care!*

Camera holds on the rubbish bin. SATURNA leans over it, takes out the slippers, throws in some more rubbish, then

---

* Cut in the editing.

puts the slippers back again.

*[The scene changes to the site of a half-built house, daytime. We hear the town clock striking midday. SATURNA's brother, LEON, straightens up from where he has been laying bricks and, putting his hands on his hips, goes towards a shady corner. The other bricklayers do the same, each choosing a place to eat their lunch. SATURNO, whose hands and overalls are covered in plaster, goes and plunges his hands into a tub of water, rubs them clean, then, after shaking the water off them, goes and sits down beside his uncle.

LEON: *Did your mother bring you something to eat?*
At the same time he makes a meaningful gesture with his hand, so that the deaf-mute can understand him. SATURNO nods and points to a saucepan beside him. LEON stretches out his arm, picks up the saucepan and takes off the lid. It is full of stew, a rather meagre stew which was no doubt left over the day before at DON LOPE's. LEON puts the lid back on the saucepan and puts it to one side, preventing SATURNO from taking it back as he had intended.

LEON: *Hold on, greedy-guts! The stew's for this evening.*
He then produces, from a small satchel, a large piece of bread, four sardines, an onion, some salt and a tomato. He gives his nephew a piece of bread and a sardine and heartily tucks in to the rest himself.

The deaf-mute does not touch his share and protests vigorously against the injustice which has been done to him. He indicates with gestures that the saucepan belongs to him and LEON must give it back.

LEON: *Shut up and eat, sonny.*
Talking with his mouth full, he articulates carefully to make himself understood to SATURNO.

LEON: *I . . . already . . . told you . . . the stew's . . . for . . . this . . . evening.*

SATURNO springs up, throws the bread and sardine down

---

* The following scene was not shot.

on his uncle's satchel and goes off towards the street in great indignation.

Another BRICKLAYER sitting near by, who has witnessed the scene, shakes his head and smiles.

BRICKLAYER with his mouth full: *You've got your hands full with a bad-tempered little sod like that for a nephew!*

Still munching, LEON tries to control his anger as he watches his nephew walk away into the distance. He turns his head towards his companion and, assuming a worldly air, exclaims:

LEON: *Huh, he's just soft! Something tells me he's not cut out for working on a site. . . . You've got to know what's what, right?*

The other BRICKLAYER nods gravely. The two men continue their meal.]

A street at night: TRISTANA and HORACIO are seen in the background, coming towards camera. A clock strikes. Close-up of the two of them. HORACIO has his arm around TRISTANA. (Still on page 72)

HORACIO: *I don't want to go by myself. I want you to come with me.*

TRISTANA: *What am I supposed to do?*

HORACIO: *I came for a month, and look how long I've stayed. I can only ask you again: leave that house and come with me.*

TRISTANA: *Give me a little more time. It's not as easy as you think.*

HORACIO: *Well, make up your mind. Everything must be settled by tomorrow.*

He kisses her on the forehead.

Reverse angle medium close-up of the two of them, in back view. Camera tracks after them as they walk along the gloomy street.

TRISTANA: *Have a little patience, my darling. Do you really think that I'm not unhappy with this life of slavery that I lead. . . . I want to be free, I want to work. I wasn't a bad pianist, you know. But when my mother died. . . . If I practised a bit and had some lessons . . . and you would work on your side. . . . Wouldn't it be marvellous!*

Long shot of a street corner. The junction forms a small square surrounded by old houses. The couple come round the corner towards us.

TRISTANA: *I'm not very well educated, you know. . . . But I think that I'm capable . . . that I would be capable of doing great things. . . . Though for little things, I'm certainly quite hopeless.*

They stop in a doorway and HORACIO leans against the wall and holds TRISTANA in his arms. They stand for a moment, cheek to cheek. He kisses her. Camera pans back to the street corner as an ageing and respectable CITIZEN of the town — probably a bureaucrat or trader — approaches. Beside him is his wife, a typical petty-bourgeoise 'lady', and following close behind them is another, younger woman, probably their daughter. Seeing the couple in the doorway, the CITIZEN brings his little party to a halt.

CITIZEN indignantly, to the couple: *There's a place for that kind of thing! . . . And it's at home, not in public.*

The trio are now standing in the foreground. In the background, HORACIO disengages himself from TRISTANA and comes threateningly towards them.

HORACIO furious: *What's that you say?*

Reverse shot of the CITIZEN and the two women, facing camera.

CITIZEN: *Can't you see there are ladies passing here? . . . Really, you might show a little more decency!*

HORACIO: *What are you blathering about?*

CITIZEN pompously: *I dislike people who treat the street as a brothel!*

Resume on HORACIO, who moves forward, even more threateningly than before. Camera pans to include the trio while TRISTANA rushes forward to hold HORACIO back. (Still on page 72)

HORACIO: *You're being extremely offensive and I'm going to . . .*

TRISTANA holds him back by the arm.

CITIZEN less sure of himself: *You can come and explain your conduct at the police station if you prefer.*

His wife intervenes in a scornful voice.
WIFE: *That's it! . . . That'll teach them to have a regard for common decency!*
TRISTANA pulls HORACIO aside with an imploring expression.
TRISTANA: *Horacio, I beg you, don't make a scene. Come away! . . . It's late.*
The CITIZEN and his women depart, while TRISTANA drags HORACIO away in the opposite direction.*

The scene changes to DON LOPE's living room, at night. SATURNA is seen in medium shot as she stands holding her employer's dressing gown, waiting as he takes off his jacket. Then she helps him on with the dressing gown.
DON LOPE: *She comes in later and later. You see what it's come to . . . now it's you who have to help me with these private chores.*
Camera pans round the room. We can see that the only remaining picture, as well as the arrangements of fencing weapons and the case of ornamental pistols, have disappeared from the wall — having no doubt been sold by DON LOPE in order to pay for the upkeep of his household. SATURNA picks up DON LOPE's shoes, hangs his jacket over her arm and waits patiently while he takes off his collar and tie.
DON LOPE: *You must know something about all this going out and all this rebellion. . . . Don't think it's an unhealthy curiosity which makes me ask you. I'm doing it for her sake, because she is still too young to know how to defend herself. And if you have some affection for her, you should tell me what you know, so that I can stamp out the evil at its root.*
Holding his clothes, SATURNA says to him, rather shortly:
SATURNA: *I don't know a thing, sir. You would do better to speak to her.*
The front door bell rings. She goes out. DON LOPE remains motionless, waiting for the sound of the door. Then he looks at his pocket watch: it can only be TRISTANA coming

---
* End of the third reel, 600 metres.

in at such a late hour. He hears whispering in the corridor.
SATURNA off : *The master wants to see you.*
TRISTANA comes in, very sure of herself, taking off her hat. She crosses the room, practically ignoring DON LOPE as she passes him.

DON LOPE : *Sit down. . . . I've got something to say to you.* She does not sit down. Tying the belt of his dressing gown, DON LOPE takes a few steps across the room to face TRISTANA.

Medium close-up of TRISTANA, impassive. Camera tracks out as DON LOPE comes close to her.

DON LOPE : *Tristana, I'm an old dog and I know that, with any girl of your age, if she rushes out into the street every day, it means she has found a bone. . . . I don't know what kind of bone it is in your case, but if you value your life don't deny it.*

TRISTANA is not in the least perturbed.

TRISTANA : *What do you want me to do? Lie to you?*

Camera follows DON LOPE as he moves across to the fireplace.

DON LOPE : *You are defending yourself badly, and that convinces me.* He looks at her threateningly. *. . . I think that up till now it has only been a matter of innocent games, because if it were otherwise . . .*

Camera tracks with him as he comes back towards her. He stares at her. TRISTANA turns her head away, unable to withstand his gaze.

DON LOPE : *As for me . . . listen to me, no one has ever humiliated me. And if you want to avoid anything worse, I can declare myself to be your father and demand that you account for your behaviour. Your mother entrusted you to me and I am resolved to protect you and defend your honour.*

TRISTANA turns round, furious at what her guardian has just said. Camera tracks in on her.

TRISTANA : *You talk to me of honour? . . . You? But it was you who took it away from me. If my mother could see what you've done to me . . .*

Medium close-up of DON LOPE.

DON LOPE : *God knows if your fate wouldn't have been worse, if you had been alone in the world or in other hands than mine.*

Pan to include the two of them, face to face.

TRISTANA: *Hypocrite!*

DON LOPE takes her by the arm and speaks to her more tenderly.

DON LOPE: *You know very well that I cannot regard you in the same way as all the other women I have known. Let me look upon you as I never have on any other woman — as a being who is dear to me ... as part of my own flesh and blood. ... What is it, don't you believe me?*

TRISTANA shrugs her shoulders scornfully and pulls away from him, going off as she speaks.

TRISTANA: *No, I don't believe you. I'm tired of hearing you always repeating the same thing.*

Pan as DON LOPE crosses the room to rejoin TRISTANA by the window.

DON LOPE: *Perhaps I've behaved badly towards you ... but now I want to be good and you've got to listen to me. I don't want to play the jealous husband or the domestic tyrant — I know how ridiculous they are, better than anyone. I won't forbid you to go out ... but I don't like it. I've spoken.*

TRISTANA moves out of frame. Camera holds on DON LOPE for a moment.

In the kitchen, we see TRISTANA in medium shot as she takes some glasses and comes and puts them down on the table. Camera tracks out in front of her as she does so, revealing the rest of the room. SATURNA is standing in front of the stove, putting some food on a plate.

SATURNA: *It's very good, Miss Tristana ... try it.*

She brings the plate over to TRISTANA in the foreground. Still standing, TRISTANA tastes the food and indicates her approval. The service bell rings; SATURNA makes as if to answer it, but TRISTANA stops her.

TRISTANA: *I'm sure it's me he's calling for. I wonder what he wants this time!* She hands the plate to SATURNA. *Here, take this.*

She goes out. Camera holds on SATURNA, who tastes the food.

Medium close-up of TRISTANA as she enters DON LOPE's

bedroom, looking very sure of herself. Camera tracks out in front of her.

TRISTANA: *What do you want now?*

DON LOPE off: *Come here, my child, come over here.*

Camera pans to reveal DON LOPE, in three-quarter back view, seated in an armchair. TRISTANA comes across and stands stiffly in front of him.

DON LOPE: *I know that I wouldn't be able to sleep if I left you angry after the conversation we had earlier. Forgive me for having upset you and . . . come now, tell me about your lover!*

Camera circles round them. While speaking, DON LOPE has gradually persuaded TRISTANA to sit on his knee.

TRISTANA shortly: *I've nothing to tell.*

DON LOPE seems resigned. He sighs.

DON LOPE: *Very well. I shall find out. Even if you behave badly towards me, I owe you such a debt of gratitude.*

He now tries to win her over by manipulating her feelings.

DON LOPE: *You have loved me in my old age. You have given me your youth. And I have treated you badly . . . but it's because I cannot convince myself that I am old.*

As he speaks, DON LOPE holds her more closely to him, and his hand begins to caress her body. He tries to kiss her, but TRISTANA pushes him away roughly (Still on page 105) and gets up, looking at him aggressively. He also gets up, with a resentful look.

DON LOPE: *I am not in the habit of insisting when I am rebuffed. Keep your juvenile charms for some fashionable young puppy. . . . But I might just lose my temper and decide to teach you a lesson. It would worry me no more than crushing an ant. . . .*

He looks at her threateningly, but TRISTANA faces up to him, furious.

TRISTANA: *Go on then; I'm not afraid of you! . . . Kill me when you like.*

She casts a furious glance at him, whirls round and goes off. DON LOPE is impressed by her reaction, and changes his tone.

DON LOPE: *You're very aggressive. That means it's true.*

He bows his head and, looking not so much sad as anxious, he goes and sits down on the edge of the bed.

Medium close-up of SATURNA in the kitchen. She is preparing some apples for cooking as TRISTANA comes in with an air of decision.

TRISTANA: *When you go to market tomorrow, tell him to wait for me in his studio. Alone if possible.*

SATURNA looks at her questioningly, in some alarm.

TRISTANA: *I shall go even if he kills me. . . . That way at least he'll have a reason for it.*

She goes out.

The scene changes to the café, in the daytime. It is full of people talking loudly amid clouds of cigarette smoke and over the cries of the waiters calling out their orders. In the background are DON LOPE's friends. We can hear their voices but the general hubbub prevents us from distinguishing any particular one. DON LOPE is on his feet, putting on his coat. He seems very preoccupied, and says goodbye to his friends in a rather absent-minded fashion.

DON LOPE: *Goodbye, gentlemen. . . .* To some others: *Goodbye.*

FRIENDS: *Goodbye.*

He goes towards the exit, greeting various other acquaintances as he passes.

Medium shot looking down the arcade outside the café, with link on the motion as DON LOPE comes out of the door. Camera tracks out in front of him as he walks towards us. Suddenly SATURNO comes up to him, carrying a sheaf of newspapers. DON LOPE looks at him absently and the deaf-mute holds out a newspaper for him to buy.

DON LOPE: *So now you're a newspaper seller! . . . That really crowns it all!*

SATURNO, who does not understand what DON LOPE has said, but has seen that he is looking for a coin, offers DON LOPE a newspaper.

DON LOPE: *No, I don't want it. . . . Here.*

He gives him the coin. SATURNO takes it and again tries to give him the paper. DON LOPE shakes his head negatively. He continues on his way, while in the background SATURNO hurries across to a fellow newspaper-vendor, also a deaf-mute, to explain what DON LOPE has done.

The scene changes to HORACIO's studio, at night.* Ten or twelve paintings are standing wrapped up in a corner. Camera tracks out as TRISTANA comes down some steps from HORACIO's bedroom, carrying some clothes. She puts them in an open suitcase which is lying on a table in the centre of the room.

TRISTANA: *When are we leaving?*

HORACIO appears and starts packing up some pictures on the table beside her.

HORACIO: *Half past three. We'll finish packing before we go to bed.*

TRISTANA casts her eyes round the room.

TRISTANA: *Is your studio bigger than this one?*
HORACIO: *Twice the size. And what's more, you can see the whole city from my balcony, and the setting sun from the bed. It's just the thing for a newly-married couple.*
TRISTANA: *For two lovers.*
HORACIO: *I've already told you I want you to be my wife.*
TRISTANA: *And I tell you that I will live with you for as long as you love me. If one day you've had enough of me . . . then it's bye-bye sweetheart, without any fuss. . . .*
HORACIO: *You remind me of that old goat. You talk just like him.*
TRISTANA: *The worst of it is that he's right about a lot of things. He's by no means stupid, believe me.*

At that moment there is a knock on the door and TRISTANA goes to open it; camera pans after her. A boy of about twelve — the caretaker's son — appears in the doorway.

LUISITO: *There's a gentleman downstairs who wants to speak to Don Horacio.*
TRISTANA: *Downstairs? Where?*
LUISITO: *He's walking up and down the street.*

---

* In the original script: 'TRISTANA is posing by the light of a naked bulb hanging from the ceiling and HORACIO is putting the finishing touches to the portrait which we saw earlier.'

TRISTANA: *And how do you know he wants to see him?*
She looks back towards HORACIO.
LUISITO: *Why, because he told me.*
TRISTANA glances out of the window, then comes back to HORACIO. She seems very anxious as to his intentions.
TRISTANA: *It's him. . . . Don't go down. . . . I'll go and speak to him. It would be much better.*
HORACIO: *No, I'm the one who must go. You stay here, it won't take long.*
He picks up his jacket and hurries towards the door, where the child is waiting.
TRISTANA almost shouting: *Horacio!*
HORACIO turning round: *Don't you move from here!*
He goes out, closing the door behind him. The child remains in the room.
Out in the street, DON LOPE is seen in medium shot. Camera pans with him as he paces to and fro in a dignified fashion in front of the building where HORACIO lives.
A closer shot of DON LOPE. He turns to face HORACIO as the latter appears at the door of the building in the background and comes straight across the dimly lit street towards him.
HORACIO: *You asked to speak to me?*
Camera circles round to show the two of them, face to face. DON LOPE looks at HORACIO disdainfully.
DON LOPE: *Tell Tristana to return home immediately. Afterwards you and I will settle this affair like gentlemen.*
HORACIO: *For a start you can get lost and stop walking up and down my street.*
DON LOPE: *I am the young lady's guardian!*
HORACIO: *Guardian indeed! She's told me what kind of a dirty old man you are.*
DON LOPE turns pale with rage. He grits his teeth and, raising the hand in which he is holding his gloves, he hits his adversary twice across the face with them. For a moment HORACIO remains rooted to the spot in astonishment.
A closer shot, with DON LOPE back to camera in the

foreground.

Don Lope haughtily: *Tomorrow you will be visited by two of my friends . . .*

He is unable to finish his sentence, for Horacio, showing a total disregard for either the code of honour or the rules of politeness, punches him as hard as he can.

Reverse shot of Don Lope as he falls over backwards and measures his length on the ground. (Still on page 105) In a nearby alley, a passer-by is seen signalling to another.

First Man: *Hey, Pepe!*

The second man comes up the alley and they both rush forward to help Don Lope.* Camera tracks out to include Horacio in the foreground. The two men cast furious looks at him as they pick up Don Lope.

First Man to Horacio: *You should be more careful. Can't you see he's an old man?*

Horacio: *Mind your own business.*

The two men support Don Lope, who is on his feet, but staggering.

First Man: *Would you like us to take you to a chemist?*

Don Lope: *No, thank you.*

Second Man: *Are you hurt?*

Don Lope: *No, I'm quite all right, thank you.*

Camera pans as the two men lead Don Lope away, passing in front of Horacio. The latter takes a few steps forward, bends down and picks up Don Lope's cane, then calls after the group.

Horacio: *Hey . . . take this.*

One of the men takes the cane and the trio go off, while Horacio comes back towards the entrance to the building.

Medium shot of the two men supporting Don Lope. Once they have turned the corner into another alleyway, Don Lope disengages himself and thanks them with a bow.

---

* The original script had another shot inserted here:
'Resume on the studio, shot from the outside. Through one of the windows, we see Tristana, who has evidently witnessed the scene in the street, as her face shows her distress at the incident.'

Don Lope: *Thank you, gentlemen . . . thank you.*
   The two men go off, and Don Lope, with his back to us and slightly bowed, walks painfully away into the night. He passes someone coming the other way.

   The scene changes to the railway station, daytime. Camera pans rapidly to the station clock, which says three-thirty.
   Medium shot of Saturna and Tristana standing on the platform, embracing, in front of a train which is about to leave. Horacio is waiting for Tristana in the doorway of one of the carriages. The train whistles. (Still on page 106)
Tristana to Saturna: *Goodbye!*
   She pulls away from Saturna and gets up into the carriage, helped by Horacio. Saturna is seen in three-quarter back view as the train starts to move.
Saturna: *Goodbye. . . . Write to me. . . . Don't forget me completely! . . . Bon voyage!*
   She waves, visibly moved by Tristana's departure. The train draws away into the distance. Camera pans with Saturna as she goes back across the railway lines towards the station building.
   Inside the station building, camera pans after Saturna as she walks across the booking hall to join Don Lope, who is waiting for her.
Saturna: *Well, that's that, sir.*
Don Lope: *She'll come back, Saturna. . . . I'm certain that she'll come back.*
   We follow Don Lope as he hurries towards the station exit, with Saturna following him a few yards behind.

THE YEAR 1933

*[The scene changes to a secluded square, in the daytime. The ground is paved with stone and there are few houses — two or three large ones which at one time must have housed families of the middle nobility and, wedged

---

* The following scene in square brackets was cut during the shooting, only the shots of the visitors' table being retained in the film. The latter are repeated in the appropriate position for the sake of clarity.

between them, a few more modest buildings. The whitewashed walls of the poorer houses contrast with the darker walls and the carved stone door and window-frames of the larger ones.

The house which takes up half of the farther end of the square seems to be the best preserved. It has wrought iron balconies on the first floor, ornamental bars on the ground floor windows, and a large doorway with a coat of arms in relief.

One side of the double door is closed, and through the other, which is half open, we can see a table covered with a black cloth. On the table is a silver salver, on which there are some visiting cards and a visitors' book. A bow of black ribbon hangs on the closed half of the door.

The DOORKEEPER is standing near the house, chatting to SATURNA. They both watch as several ladies and gentlemen go in or come out of the house. The gentlemen wear black frock coats and the ladies black silk dresses and mantillas.

DOORKEEPER: *Look at 'em all — the upper crust coming to pay their respects.*

SATURNA is accompanied by SATURNO; she nods, also impressed by the visitors' appearance.

SATURNA: *What time did she die?*

DOORKEEPER: *In the early morning. The fun started yesterday evening! . . . No one in the house has had a wink of sleep.*

SATURNO says something in sign language. SATURNA translates.

SATURNA: *He says that, rich or poor, we'll all have to go feet first one day.*

The DOORKEEPER agrees. Someone calls from inside the house.

A VOICE: *Porter!*

DOORKEEPER to SATURNA: *Excuse me.*

He goes off. SATURNA watches him go, then moves away rapidly with her son.]

As the sequence starts, we see a table draped in black through a half-open door. On the table is a silver salver on which there are some visiting cards, a large book intended for the signatures and condolences of the visitors, and an ink-stand. A black-gloved hand signs the book. Camera tilts up to show a woman dressed in mourning. She moves away. A very smartly dressed man signs in his turn. Tilt down to show his hands.

Exterior shot of the street. Three very elegant-looking women, dressed in mourning, come towards us. Other people are following them, amongst whom we recognise Don Cosme. Camera pans to show the doorway of Dona Josefina's imposing residence. The people enter the house to sign the book. The Doorkeeper is standing by the doorway.

Medium shot of the upper windows of Don Lope's house. Camera tilts down to the doorway as Don Lope comes out, looking very distinguished in a frock coat and a black tie and hat. As he walks across the small square, Don Cosme appears in the background.

Don Cosme: *Hey, Lope!*

He hurries across and shakes Don Lope by the hand.

Don Cosme: *I was just coming to see you. . . . Even knowing what you must be thinking, I feel it is my duty as a friend to come and offer you my condolences.*

Don Lope: *Thank you very much, but you know very well that we couldn't stand the sight of each other.*

Don Cosme: *Of course, Lope. . . . But even so, she was your sister.*

Don Lope has taken his friend by the arm and they now start to walk on.

Medium close-up of the two of them, camera tracking out as they walk.

Don Lope: *Do you think that otherwise I would go to the funeral, which will be nothing but a parade of cassocks? . . . After all, I remember my childhood and . . .*

Something seems to strike him as funny and he smiles to himself.

Don Lope: *The poor old girl must have been sorry to leave me behind — alive and sinning.*

Cosme stops him.

Don Cosme in reproachful tones: *Do you really think that*

Josefina could have thought of anything else but making her peace with God?

They walk on, camera tracking out in front of them again.

Don Lope: *She certainly thought of other matters as well ... more down-to-earth ones. ... Listen, Cosme, even parents — if they could take what they had when they died, their children would find themselves without a penny.*

Cosme stops him again.

Don Cosme: *The things you say! ... At any rate, I'm happy for your sake. Having endured all these hardships, you can now live in comfort.*

Don Lope ironically: *That's it, that's it! ... The dead six feet under and the living ...*

Don Cosme indignantly: *Really, Lope!*

He takes him by the arm.

Don Lope shaking free: *Leave me alone!*

Don Cosme trying to hold back his friend: *For God's sake! ...*

They go off, still arguing.

[The scene changes to Don Lope's kitchen, at night. Saturna, in a black dress and a white apron, is setting out the coffee things on a tray. The service is in silver, and the single cup of fine porcelain. She polishes the service, and we can see that she is anxious at the idea of handling such precious objects. She pours the steaming coffee into the coffee pot and goes out of the room.]*

In the dining room, camera pans from a very fine silver dinner service to reveal the rest of the room. One or two of the poorer pieces of furniture which we saw previously have been replaced by more luxurious ones. There is a lot of silver on the sideboard and, on the tablecloth, the dishes, the cutlery and the glasses etc. all bear witness to Don Lope's new-found prosperity. There is evidence of his recent inheritance everywhere. We hear him talking to himself.

---

* This section was not shot.

Don Lope off: *You remember I had to sell it all? Well, I went and bought it back from that same old Jew.* . . . *He chuckles, then murmurs to himself:* Tristana . . . Triste-ana.*

Camera arrives at the table, where there is a bottle of champagne in an ice-bucket. Don Lope is flushed with all the good food he has eaten and also slightly drunk.

Don Lope: *Right. No more drinking for tonight.* . . . *A little drop more and it's all gone.*

He pours himself a glass of champagne and, looking at the place where Tristana used to sit, offers her a drink with a glazed expression.

Don Lope: *Here, drink up, woman.* . . . *You don't want it?* . . . *So much the better. I'll drink it myself.*

He laughs, swallows the contents of the glass, and pours himself another.

Shot of Don Lope from another angle as Saturna approaches and puts down the tray on the table in order to serve the coffee. He is sprawled in his chair, lighting a cigarette. Saturna looks anxious and hesitant.

Saturna *pouring the coffee*: *Sir . . . there's something I must tell you.* . . . *He looks at her blankly.* I've kept it to myself for two days. . . . As you're bound to find out in the end, the sooner you know the better. . . . Miss Tristana is back.

In his present state, Don Lope has some difficulty in grasping the news. He gazes at Saturna.

Don Lope: *Tristana?*

Saturna: *Yes, sir.*

Don Lope looks pensive for a moment as he begins to realise what this means as far as he is concerned.

Don Lope: *And . . . what's she come back for?*

Saturna: *You'll have to ask Mr. Horacio that.*

On hearing the name of the painter, Don Lope reacts as if to an unpleasant surprise.

Don Lope: *What?* . . . *She's come with that fellow?*

Saturna: *Yes, sir . . . and he says that he would like to speak to you.*

---

* This is a play on words. ' Triste ' in Spanish means ' sad '.

Don Lope: *I have nothing to say.* . . . *If they want something, she can come and see me herself.*
Saturna: *If only she could!* . . . *She's ill.*

Don Lope looks at her interrogatively.

Saturna: *She's in a bad way, sir* . . . *very bad. You haven't seen her for two years. She's changed a lot, poor thing.*

The old man sits gazing at the empty champagne glass which he is holding, torn by conflicting sentiments. Then he reacts, suddenly and violently. He gets up and, trying to walk straight, goes towards the door.

Don Lope: *I'll go.*

Camera pans as he goes out of the room, followed by Saturna.

The scene changes to the entrance hall of a hotel, at night. It is a comfortable, second-class establishment, with no pretensions. At first we see the reception counter, with pigeon-holes for the residents' correspondence. The receptionist is putting a ledger book into his briefcase. Camera pans to show the bottom of the staircase as Horacio comes down, looking very smart and respectable. He has now grown a moustache. He moves towards the lounge adjoining the hall and goes up to Don Lope, who is standing by the fireplace. Horacio confronts his visitor with an air of decision, but respectfully none the less. He holds out his hand, but Don Lope does not take it.

Horacio in a low voice: *First of all I must ask you to forgive me for my conduct when we last met.*

The old man does not reply and looks at him with a severe, almost disdainful expression; Horacio is somewhat disconcerted. He makes as if to speak, but Don Lope stops him with a gesture, indicating the staircase. Horacio turns.

Low angle shot of the receptionist as he goes up the stairs and out of sight. A pause. Camera pans back to the two men. (Still on page 106)

Horacio: *I am ready to give you satisfaction in whatever manner you wish, at a place of your choosing.*

Don Lope makes a scornful gesture.

Don Lope: *That's of no interest now.*

Horacio: *Do please sit down.*

The two of them sit down in large leather armchairs, facing each other in front of the fireplace, where a log fire is blazing.

Horacio: *I have asked Tristana to marry me several times. She has always refused....* Camera moves towards Horacio. *I may not be rich, but she has never had to go without anything.... We have been quite happy together, but now she is ill, perhaps incurably so.*

Don Lope off: *What's the matter with her?*

Horacio: *She has a tumour on her leg. She's been in pain for weeks.*

Close-up of Don Lope, who has difficulty in concealing his agitation and distress.

Horacio off: *It's sheer purgatory for her.*

Don Lope: *Have you seen a doctor?*

Close-up of Horacio. He nods, takes a piece of paper out of his jacket pocket and gets up and gives it to Don Lope. Camera pans to include the latter.

Horacio: *Here's the diagnosis.*

Don Lope reads it, then folds up the paper and hands it back to Horacio.

Don Lope: *I don't understand a word of that gibberish!... Why have you brought her back here?*

For the first time, Horacio reveals his agitation as he speaks.

Horacio: *It was she who insisted on coming. She nearly drove me crazy until I agreed.*

Very agitated, Horacio walks nervously across to the fireplace and leans on the mantelpiece.

Horacio: *She thinks she's going to die.... She still thinks of you as ...* He hesitates ... *her father. She says that she wants to die in your house.*

Don Lope: *What if I won't have her?*

Horacio: *I shall take her back with me. I'm not trying to get rid of her.*

Don Lope still seems slightly doubtful.

Don Lope: *If I open my house to Tristana ... what about*

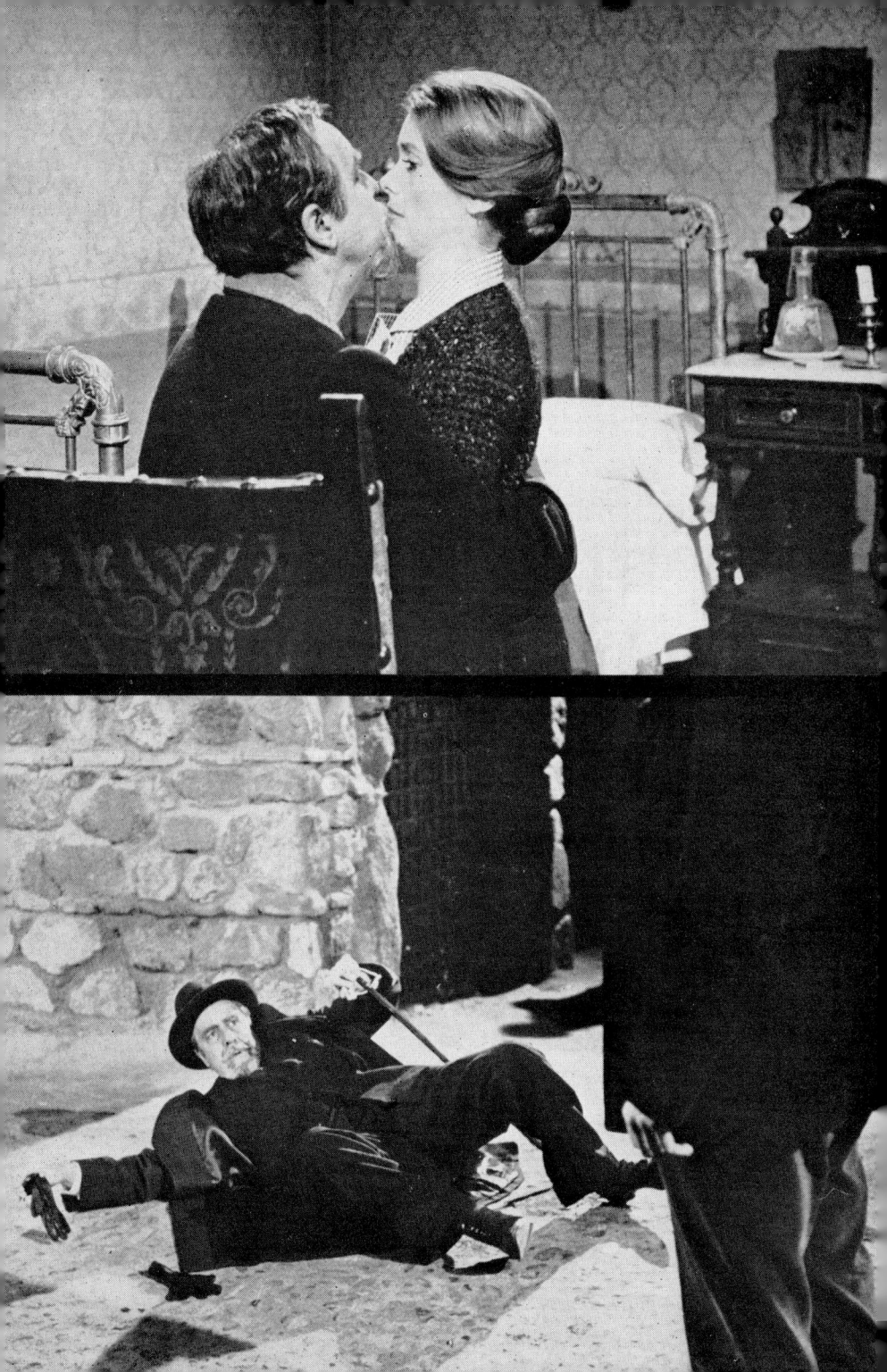

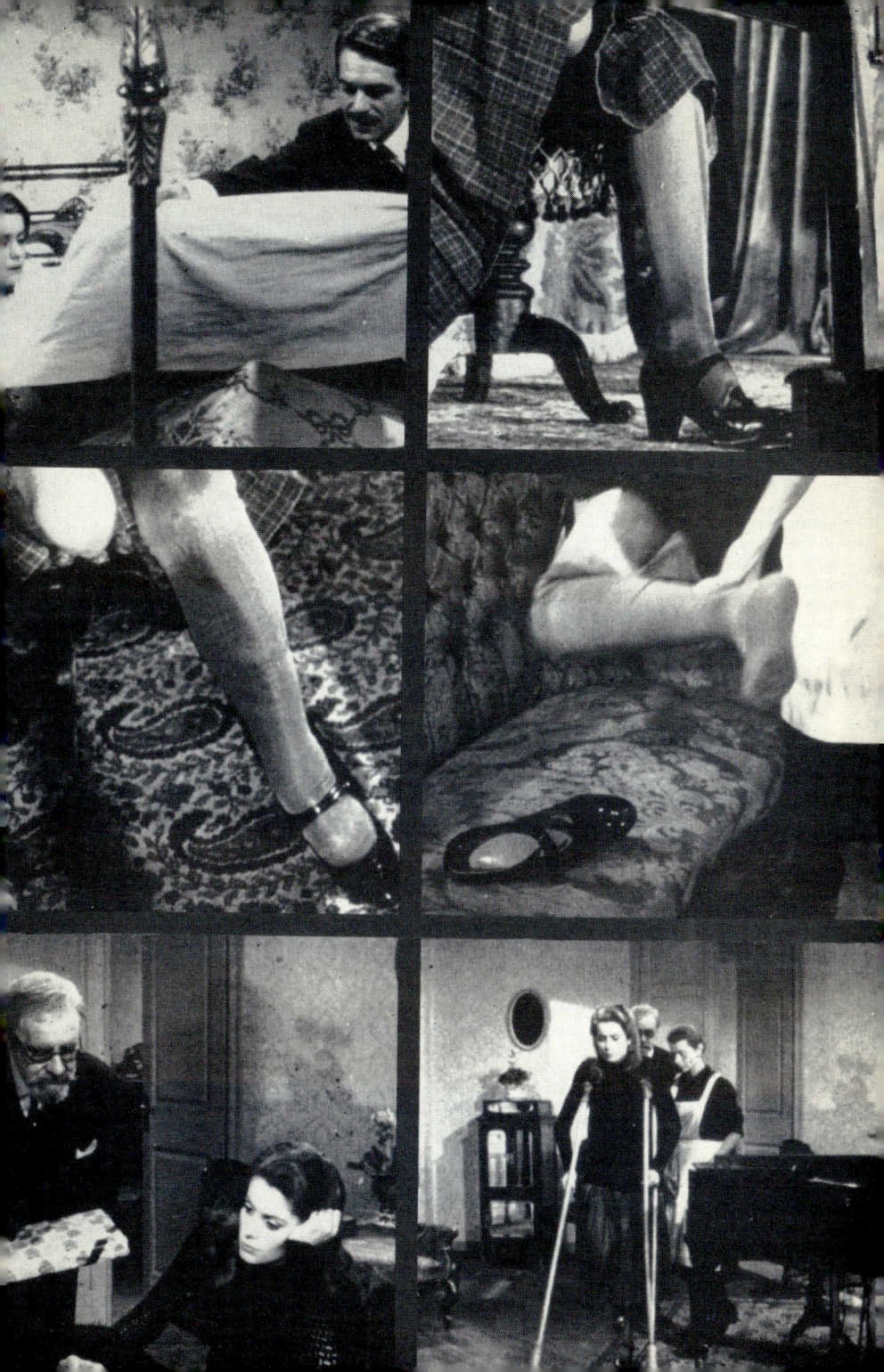

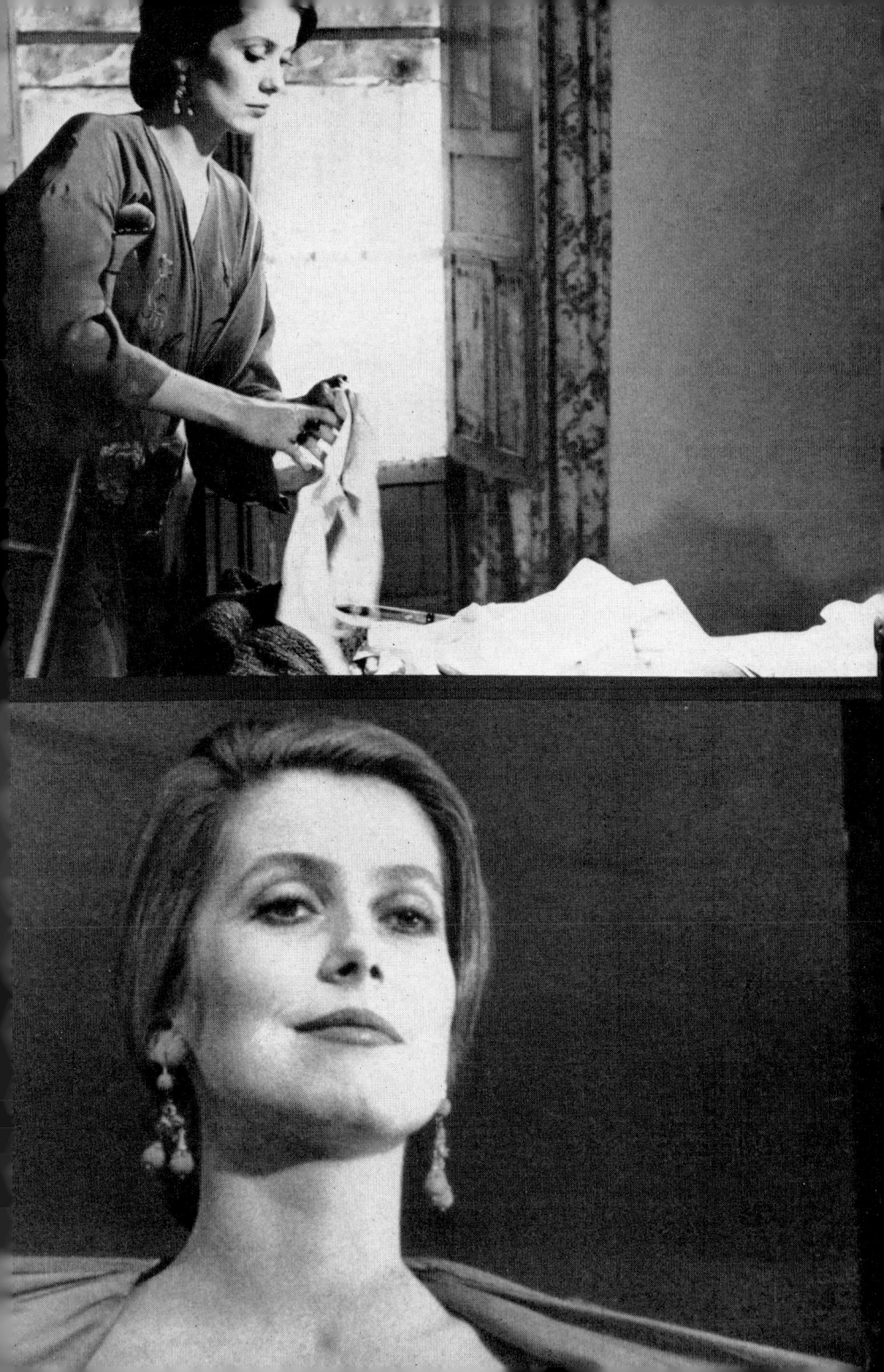

you, what will you do?
HORACIO *coming towards* DON LOPE : *I shall remain in the town and await . . . developments. Of course I would not be so tactless as to impose my presence on you.*

After a short pause, DON LOPE makes up his mind.
DON LOPE : *You can tell her that I shall come and collect her tomorrow with Saturna.*

Medium close-up of the two men. Without further comment, and ignoring HORACIO, who bows his head in assent, DON LOPE departs, leaving the painter somewhat surprised by this sudden dénouement.
[In the street outside, SATURNA stands looking nervous and impatient, trying to see what is happening inside the hotel without letting herself be seen.]*
Medium shot of DON LOPE, who comes out of the hotel, walking very fast as though he wanted to get away from there as quickly as possible. SATURNA hurries forward and runs after him. As he says nothing, she asks anxiously :
SATURNA : *What happened?*
DON LOPE *overjoyed* : *This time she won't escape, Saturna. . . . If she comes into my house, she will never leave it again. Come on.*

He lays a hand on SATURNA's shoulder and the two of them walk up the street, away from camera. They pass a municipal night watchman, who greets them as they go by.

The scene changes to DON LOPE's living room, in the daytime. DON LOPE is showing four removals men where to put down a grand piano which they are carrying. SATURNO, neatly dressed as a footman, moves to and fro, trying to make himself useful. DON LOPE, very much the master of the house, gives a smile of satisfaction as the piano is placed in position.
DON LOPE *to the removals men* : *A little further back, please. . . . There . . . that's fine.*

He tips the men generously and they thank him profusely.

---
* This section was not shot.

REMOVALS MEN: *Thank you, sir. . . . Oh thank you. . . . At your service, sir. . . .*
> At this point we notice a young DOCTOR, seated at the table, writing out a prescription. The removals men go out. In the background, SATURNO goes up to the piano and dusts it off. DON LOPE goes up to the DOCTOR.

DON LOPE: *Well, Doctor?*
DR. MIQUIS: *Just a moment.*
> DON LOPE walks round the room, now full of concern.
> We move to the interior of TRISTANA's bedroom, which has been refurnished in accordance with DON LOPE's new financial status.* The results bear witness to his affection for his ward: there are expensive carpets and curtains, new furniture, very feminine and gay, a folding screen, and china and glass ornaments. The bedstead is of polished brass, decorated with flowers and arabesques. The sequence starts on a medium shot of SATURNA standing near the bed as she wraps a hot brick in some linen.

SATURNA: *This will warm it up nicely and it won't hurt so much.*
TRISTANA wearily, off: *Nothing will make it any better, Saturna. . . . Oh! . . . It hurts!*
> SATURNA carefully arranges the bedclothes.

SATURNA: *Bah! . . . No one ever died from a pain in the knee.*
> As she says these words, she goes towards the head of the bed, and camera follows her to reveal TRISTANA lying there, resting. Her eyes are closed, but she is evidently not asleep as her features are slightly contracted in a grimace of physical pain. She is very thin and pale, and we see that she has developed as a woman. SATURNA slips the brick between the sheets. At this point DON LOPE enters the room with SATURNO. He goes to the head of the bed while SATURNO remains at its foot, making affectionate gestures in TRISTANA's direction.

DON LOPE: *How are you, dearest? Better, aren't you? Saturno's come to pay you a little visit. . . . Doctor Miquis says that*

---

* This general description is taken from the original script.

you're doing well and the sharp pain is a sign that it's getting better.

Tristana *smiles sceptically and looks at* Saturno.

Don Lope: *Off you go now, Saturno.*

Saturno *waves goodbye to* Tristana, *who does the same in return. He goes out.* Don Lope *goes round to the other side of the bed.*

Don Lope: *Keep your spirits up! . . . In a month's time you'll be able to jump up and down . . . and even dance the malagueña!*

Tristana: *You just say that to console me . . . but I know that I shall never be able to dance again.*

Don Lope: *Come come now, there's nothing to worry about! I'm convinced that all will be well . . . so you must be convinced too. . . .*

As he speaks, camera tracks in on the two of them. Saturna *is partly visible on the other side of the bed.*

Don Lope: *The piano you wanted so much has just arrived. It's in the living room. Now we shall see if you have really made all the progress you've been boasting about.*

He pats her on the arm.

Tristana: *I shall never be able to play again, Lope.*

Don Lope: *Don't be silly, you don't play the piano with your legs. . . . Come on, keep your pecker up. . . .*

Camera tracks in towards Tristana.

Tristana: *What, with this terrible pain?*

Don Lope: *I told you, it's a good sign if it hurts. It means the reaction is beginning.*

Tristana *clearly does not believe him. She turns her head away sadly.*

[Don Lope: *Would you like to have news of a certain person? Because if you wish, and if it will do you good, I would be prepared to go and fetch him.*

Tristana: *It makes me feel ashamed — you being so good, when I'm so . . .*

Don Lope: *Just think that I'm no longer the man I was and that I love you differently . . . as a friend or however you wish. Just that and nothing more! . . . It has taken me a long time to appreciate your worth, but it's never too late to*

do good. I admit that I am not worthy of advising you, and if I do give you advice it is disinterested. You can take it or leave it, just as it suits you.
TRISTANA: *But how can he come if you're here?*
DON LOPE: *Do you think that I'm that stupid? . . . Have I not always been discreet? . . . If he comes, you may be sure that I shall be out when he does so.*]*

>Medium shot of DR. MIQUIS, whom SATURNO has just ushered into the bedroom. His manner is affable and even jovial.

DR. MIQUIS: *And how's my favourite patient today?*
TRISTANA off: *Worse than ever, Doctor.*

>Camera pans as the DOCTOR approaches the bed. He addresses DON LOPE and SATURNA, as well as SATURNO, who is hovering in the doorway.

DR. MIQUIS: *Would you leave me alone with her, please.*

>They all go out. The door closes behind them. The DOCTOR puts his bag down on a table and comes back towards the bed.

DR. MIQUIS: *How are you feeling, Tristanita?*
TRISTANA: *I was very feverish all last night. . . .* A pause, then she says anxiously: *I'm in a bad way, aren't I?*

>The DOCTOR draws back the bedclothes. (Still on page 107)

TRISTANA: *Tell me the truth.*
DR. MIQUIS: *I've already told you several times. Your case is very common. It's painful, of course, but that will soon ease off.*

>Camera follows him as he passes to the other side of the bed, coming into back view in the foreground, and examines the affected leg (her right one), which we cannot see.

TRISTANA: *A few days ago, I still thought it was marvellous to be alive. Now I think that it's better to die.*

>She cries out in pain as the DOCTOR touches her leg.
>In the living room, DON LOPE is walking to and fro, looking very downcast. The forced gaiety which he assumed in talking to TRISTANA has given way to depression.

---

* Cut in the editing.

SATURNA is polishing the piano while SATURNO looks on in the background.

DON LOPE: *I think she's in a very bad way, Saturna.*

SATURNA: *If you'd let me give her a camomile and cow-dung poultice she would be better by now.*

DON LOPE: *Don't be a fool!*

Camera tracks in on him as he comes towards the piano. The DOCTOR enters the room and approaches DON LOPE. The two of them walk round the room as they talk.

DR. MIQUIS: *Don Lope, my friend, things have got to the point which I was afraid of. . . . Tristana is very ill. . . . I feel obliged to speak plainly to a man of your fibre.*

DON LOPE: *Go on.*

DR. MIQUIS: *There's been a reabsorption . . . it's getting into the blood. We shall have to operate.*

They halt. DON LOPE, who has his hand in the front of his jacket in a Napoleonic fashion, nods in agreement, but the DOCTOR realises that he has not entirely grasped the meaning of the word ' operate '.

DR. MIQUIS insistently: *Her leg will have to come off.*

DON LOPE seems to age a little more as he hears these words. He has difficulty in standing.

DON LOPE: *The poor child! . . . That's frightful! . . . To mutilate her so horribly . . . when?*

DR. MIQUIS: *If we lose a day it may be too late.*

DON LOPE: *What a terrible thing your science is, Doctor, when it cannot cure people without carving them up!*

Camera pans as DON LOPE goes towards SATURNA, who has remained by the piano in silent horror and amazement.

DON LOPE: *Saturna . . . go to her. She mustn't be left alone! . . .*

SATURNA crosses the room and goes off. DON LOPE comes back to the DOCTOR and takes him by the arm.

DON LOPE faintly, almost gibbering: *Doctor, try and find another way. . . You can cut both my legs off straight away if it will do any good.*

Seeing that DON LOPE has lost control of himself, the DOCTOR moves away, shrugging his shoulders. DON LOPE takes off his glasses.

DON LOPE: *Forgive me, Doctor . . . I don't know what I'm saying any more. . . . I'm out of my mind. . . . Do what you feel you have to.*

Medium shot of the DOCTOR standing by the table. He puts a note in an envelope.

DR. MIQUIS: *I shall be assisted by my friend Dr. Ruiz Alonso, who is a surgeon of some repute. . . . Send this note to his house at once. I think that if the amputation is successful we may be able to save her.*

DON LOPE, who has now come into shot, takes the note from him.

DON LOPE: *May be able? . . . Does that mean that even so you are not sure?*

DR. MIQUIS: *Science is not infallible, unfortunately . . . and this might be the moment to have recourse to other sources . . . of healing. I know from experience how much it can help for the patient to have a clear conscience. So I would suggest that you call a priest this very day, to take her confession and . . .*

Camera pans with DON LOPE as he walks around the room. He reacts violently to such a proposition.

DON LOPE vehemently: *A priest in my house? . . . Never! I appreciate your advice but I cannot accept it . . .* [*and I do not consider myself an atheist. I would even say that my faith is worth more than that of quite a few of your over-fed churchmen. I believe in Christ as a preacher. . . .*]* *I know that Christ was the first socialist etc. etc. . . . Well, so what? The real priests are people like us, people who defend the innocent, the enemies of hypocrisy, injustice and filthy lucre!*

DR. MIQUIS comes up to him, smiles and goes towards TRISTANA's room. He gives DON LOPE a friendly pat on the shoulder as he passes.

DR. MIQUIS: *I'm going to see her for a moment.*

He goes out of frame, and camera holds on DON LOPE. His energy has dissolved away and depression overtakes him again. He sits down. SATURNO comes up to him sadly

---

* Not heard in the version screened.

and tries to 'speak' to him in sign language. DON LOPE gets up and puts his arm round SATURNO's shoulders. The latter, realising his master's distress, pats him comfortingly on the back. They walk towards the back of the room, SATURNO gesturing away.

The scene changes to the interior of the café. The noisy activity we saw there previously has given way to calm and silence. It is the middle of the morning and business is slack. [At the counter, the only WAITER on duty picks up a tray with a cup of white coffee and a roll on it and carries it across to a table near the window which looks out onto the street. At the table we find HORACIO, with the bored expression of someone who doesn't know what to do. He knocks on the window to call a BOOTBLACK, who runs up immediately. We see him come into the café.]* The sequence starts on a high angle medium close-up of the BOOTBLACK as he polishes HORACIO's boots. Camera tilts up to show the latter, who is reading a newspaper. The BOOTBLACK finishes his job; HORACIO gets up and pays him.

BOOTBLACK: *Thank you.*

HORACIO sits down again at the table, where his coffee has already been served. In the background, DON LOPE enters the café with a purposeful step and comes towards HORACIO's table. At first HORACIO does not notice him and DON LOPE is already standing beside his table by the time he looks up, so that he finds himself in a somewhat embarrassing situation. He gets up.

DON LOPE: *Good morning. Don't think this meeting is a matter of chance. I know that you often come to this café and I wanted to speak to you.*

HORACIO: *Please sit down.*

DON LOPE sits down beside HORACIO, who does likewise. HORACIO gestures to the WAITER.

DON LOPE: *No, I won't have anything. Thank you.*

HORACIO waves the WAITER away again. Camera tracks

---
* Not retained in the final edited version.

in on them.

DON LOPE: *Do you intend to stay here for long?*

HORACIO: *Until I know what happens to* TRISTANA, *I can't leave* . . .

He stops in mid-sentence, not quite sure whether this is quite the right moment to refer to TRISTANA. However, DON LOPE does not seem in the least bit put out, and remains quite calm.

Medium close-up of DON LOPE, with HORACIO back to camera.

DON LOPE: *Ah, yes, my dear sir! . . . You know all about her condition. . . . It's frightful! . . . She was so graceful . . . and now she's disabled for ever. You will understand my grief, since my affection for her is so deep, so pure and disinterested. . . . That is why I would like to make life pleasant for her. . . . The fact is, she is of such a changeable disposition, and now she needs you. . . .*

Reverse angle close-up of HORACIO. He leans forward.

HORACIO: *Are you trying to make fun of me? This is just an old man's fantasy. Tristana's feelings are not as changeable as you would like to think.*

Camera tracks out to include DON LOPE.

DON LOPE: *There are some things which you are too young to understand, but let us not quarrel over such a trifle. . . .*

He taps his fingers on the table in a worldly fashion, then pauses for a moment as he sees HORACIO's gaze fixed on him.

HORACIO: *Well . . . what do you want of me?*

DON LOPE: *I want you to go and see her. . . .*

The painter was obviously not expecting this invitation and he is so surprised by it that he quite loses his aplomb.

DON LOPE: *I'm not a monster. Feelings change. . . . That's how I noticed she was missing something. . . . And I'm certain that it's you. . . . Go and see her . . . every day.*

HORACIO: *It will be horribly embarrassing for me . . .*

DON LOPE: *You can go in the afternoon, from four to six. I usually take a walk at that time.*

DON LOPE gets up, bringing the conversation to a close. He puts on his hat and moves away. HORACIO gets up.

HORACIO: *Thank you, Don Lope.*
DON LOPE turning back: *Don't thank me. I'm doing it for her.*

> DON LOPE walks towards the revolving door and goes out while HORACIO sits down again, looking anxious and worried.*
> Medium close-up of HORACIO as he sits down. He picks up a pencil and begins to scribble on a piece of paper.
> [During this conversation we have seen a young man of about the same age as HORACIO sit down at one of the tables. Now, as soon as DON LOPE's back is turned, he comes over to join HORACIO.

RICARDO: *I saw you talking to him. He's got to be seen to be believed.*

> HORACIO is still recovering from the shock of the interview. He is unable to conceal his astonishment.

HORACIO: *Do you know what he came to ask me? . . . To go and see her.*

> Apparently assessing the possible consequences of his friend's conversation with DON LOPE, RICARDO is very cutting.

RICARDO: *The best thing you can do is come back with me. I'm off tomorrow.*
HORACIO: *I can't. . . . It's become a question of integrity. . . . How can I possibly leave her?*
RICARDO: *The fact is . . . to tell you the truth, a woman in that state . . .*
HORACIO: *I still love her. . . . It's not the same as before, of course, but . . .*

> His friend gestures impatiently, almost in disgust.

RICARDO: *Frankly, if it were me . . .*

> He stops in mid-sentence to hail the WAITER.

RICARDO: *Hey, you, let's have some coffee! . . .*

> And from the friend's gesture as he calls the WAITER, and HORACIO's worried face, we pass to the street where DON LOPE lives.]**

---

* End of the fourth reel, 600 metres.
** Cut during the shooting.

Medium shot of DON LOPE walking along the street with measured tread. The confectioner, LUCAS, sees him passing from inside his shop. DON LOPE stops in front of the window and looks in. LUCAS opens the door.

LUCAS: *I've got in some marrons glacés for the señorita. Do you want to take them for her?*

DON LOPE: *No . . . no, thank you. I'm not going home for the moment. I'll come by and pick them up later.*

LUCAS: *As you wish.*

DON LOPE goes on his way, camera tracking sideways with him.

Another similar shot of DON LOPE. He stops, listens for a moment and then looks up. Through the open window of the living room of his apartment we hear someone playing Chopin's Revolutionary Study on the piano. Camera tilts up, following his gaze, to show the window from below. Then it tilts down to show DON LOPE again; he walks on, passing his own front door without a glance. The music continues.

Inside DON LOPE's living room, we see TRISTANA's hands as she plays the piano.

Medium close-up of TRISTANA's legs under the piano. Her right leg is cut off above the knee and the other leg is dressed in a fine silk stocking and an expensive-looking patent leather shoe. (Still on page 107)

We now see her face as she plays. She looks extremely beautiful, her hair is carefully done and she is wearing a very handsome pair of diamond earrings.

Medium shot of the room. TRISTANA sits at the piano, facing us, while behind her HORACIO stands a little way away, listening to her playing and glancing at his watch. Camera pans as he goes over and shuts the window, comes towards TRISTANA, walks round the piano, scarcely concealing his impatience, and finally sits down beside her as she continues to play. A pause. She suddenly stops playing.

TRISTANA: *When will you be back?*

HORACIO: *In a month at the latest.*

Close-up of TRISTANA's fingers as she starts to play again.

Resume on the two of them, HORACIO in profile in the foreground. She stops playing again.

TRISTANA: *Do you mind if I tell you something?*
HORACIO: *No.*
TRISTANA: *I think that if you really loved me you wouldn't have brought me here.*
HORACIO beginning to get annoyed: *I didn't bring you here! . . . It was you who insisted on coming. . . . You said you were going to die.*
TRISTANA: *But I'm still alive.*
HORACIO: *That's the limit! You're being completely unfair!*
TRISTANA: *Perhaps . . .*

She pauses, then, leaning her elbow on the piano, lets out a thought which seems to obsess her.

TRISTANA: *Don Lope would never have taken me to another man's house.*

HORACIO listens in astonishment. Feeling that everything is quite beyond his comprehension, he gets up, camera tilting with him.

HORACIO: *Sometimes when I listen to you I can't believe that it's you who is speaking. You seem to have changed!*

High angle medium close-up of TRISTANA's legs.

TRISTANA off: *Naturally . . . I have changed! . . .*

In an access of bitterness, she draws back her skirt to show him the stump. (Still on page 107)

TRISTANA off: *How could I stay the same with this?*

Low angle shot of HORACIO, who looks at her, distressed and embarrassed.

High angle shot of her sitting at the piano. Seeing his distress, she lowers her skirt again and apologises lightly.

TRISTANA: *I'm sorry if I was brutal. . . . It would be better if you were to leave now.*

Track out to include HORACIO. He does not reply. He is obviously dying to go, even if he doesn't dare to say so. He looks at his watch.

TRISTANA: *I hope your exhibition will be a success. I really do.*

He thanks her with a gesture which is intended to be affectionate.

HORACIO: *I've still got a lot of things to do. I'll come and say*

goodbye tomorrow.
TRISTANA: *As you wish.*

HORACIO comes up to her and kisses her on the forehead. She immediately starts playing again, very loudly. Track out as he picks up his hat and coat from the sofa, glances back at TRISTANA and goes out of the door. Camera holds on TRISTANA as she continues to play.

*[As soon as he approaches her, TRISTANA throws herself into his arms and gives him a long, passionate kiss. Then she murmurs in a faraway voice:

TRISTANA: *Take me to my room! Carry me!*
HORACIO: *Now?*
TRISTANA: *Yes . . . now!*

HORACIO picks her up in his arms and carries her slowly towards the door. TRISTANA's attitude is one of total abandon. Her eyes are closed, her mouth open, her lips moist.

Outside in the corridor, HORACIO carries TRISTANA to her room and goes in.

Interior shot of the room. As he crosses the threshold, he stops for a moment to look at her. Her eyes are closed and her breath comes in gasps. Her right arm is around HORACIO's neck. He presses her against him and, for the first time since her operation, actually feels the absence of his mistress's right leg. This triggers off a strange feeling in him — a mixture of repugnance and desire. He carries her towards the bed.

Shot from HORACIO's point of view: we approach the bed. Several female garments lie in disorder on the bedspread. Amongst the silk and lace underwear we see an artificial leg, the lower part of which is perfectly shaped and clad in a fine silk stocking and a charming little patent leather shoe. The part corresponding to the thigh, however, is a mass of aluminium, straps and padding.

Shot of HORACIO's face. He looks at the apparatus, then his gaze returns to the face of his mistress, whom he lays gently on the bed.]

---

* The following section was cut as a result of modifications made during the shooting.

Medium shot of the confectioner's shop in the street outside. Don Lope comes out carrying a box tied up with a red ribbon. Camera tracks out as he crosses the square, then pans to show the doorway of his house, from which Horacio emerges, looking rather foolish, putting on his gloves. He passes Don Lope, who turns away as he does so. Horacio hurries out of shot, while Don Lope goes into the house.

Slightly high angle shot of the sofa in Don Lope's living room, on which lies a black shoe belonging to Tristana. Saturna comes partly into view as she lays down Tristana's artificial leg on the sofa. (Still on page 107)

Saturna off at first: *You ought to put it on and try and get used to it.*

Camera tilts up to show Saturna's face.

Tristana off: *Oh, no . . . it hurts too much!*

In the background, Don Lope enters carrying his box of marrons glacés. Pan as he comes up to Tristana, who is sitting leaning on the piano. Her crutches are propped against the side of it. Saturna can also be seen in the background. (Still on page 107)

Don Lope offering the box to Tristana: *So he's finally going?*
Tristana: *Yes, tomorrow.*
Don Lope: *When is he coming back?*
Tristana: *Perhaps never.*

Don Lope remains impassive, although he is obviously pleased at this possibility.

Don Lope indicating the box of sweets: *Here, take this. I know you like them.*
Tristana: *Marrons glacés?*
Don Lope nodding: *Uh huh!*
Tristana: *Thank you.*
Don Lope stroking her hair: *You're looking very lovely . . . lovelier every day.*
Tristana: *Don't make fun of me.*

He takes her hand in his.

Don Lope sincerely: *You know that I am incapable of it. You look upon the fact that you have only one leg as a disadvantage, and yet you're perhaps even more desirable than before. At least for a lot of people. . . .* He half smiles and goes to get her crutches. *I remember there was a woman in Paris when I was young. She could often be seen taking a walk along the boulevards on her crutches. She always had three or four men following her.*

TRISTANA gazes into space, while DON LOPE picks up the crutches.

TRISTANA: *There's no accounting for people's tastes.*

SATURNA: *Your bath is ready, Miss Tristana. Would you like me to give you a rub down first?*

DON LOPE mockingly: *Rub down? . . . You mean give her a massage, woman!*

SATURNA shrugs. DON LOPE holds out the crutches to TRISTANA, who gets up, and walks towards camera followed by SATURNA. (Still on page 107) They go off. DON LOPE remains by the piano. He slowly undoes his necktie and hurries off towards his study.

*[In the bathroom, we see SATURNO enter with a pitcher of hot water. He empties it into the tub, which is almost full. Shortly afterwards, TRISTANA appears in the doorway, helped by DON LOPE and SATURNA. DON LOPE and SATURNO withdraw; SATURNA shuts the door and starts to undress her young mistress.

We next see DON LOPE in his study, where he fills his pipe from a small stoneware tobacco jar standing on a small table.

Shot of the corridor. In carrying the jugs, SATURNO has spilt some water near the bathroom door. He now appears with a cloth and kneels down to mop up the water. His head is on the same level as the keyhole of the bathroom door, and fairly near to it. At that moment, DON LOPE comes out of his study and stops for a moment to light his pipe; he notices the presence of the deaf-mute. He frowns and goes towards him with an angry gesture.

DON LOPE: *What are you looking at down there?*

SATURNO smiles uncomprehendingly. In order to confirm his entirely unjustified suspicions, DON LOPE bends down

---

* The following section was cut during the shooting.

and looks through the keyhole.

Shot of TRISTANA naked in the bathtub, as seen by DON LOPE through the keyhole. SATURNA is soaping her back.

Resume on the corridor. DON LOPE straightens up and seizes SATURNO by the ear. The latter, extremely surprised, protests against the injustice of it all. DON LOPE drags him to the front door and opens it.

DON LOPE: *Out, you barefaced little wretch!*

SATURNO gestures energetically against the enormity of DON LOPE's injustice, thinking no doubt that it is a case of the pot calling the kettle black. But it doesn't do him much good. DON LOPE pushes him out and closes the door on him.]

THE YEAR 1935

Exterior shot of a small square. Everything is covered in a thick layer of snow. A couple wearing overcoats hurry across the square. Camera pans to show the porch of a church, in front of which DON LOPE is walking to and fro, well wrapped up against the cold. People come out of the church, the last to do so being TRISTANA in a luxurious wheelchair pushed by SATURNO, with SATURNA following behind.* Several months have passed. DON LOPE has lost the little sprightliness which he still had when we last saw him. Now he is an old man who no longer tries to conceal his age. He is wearing a big scarf which partly covers his face, with a beret on his head. TRISTANA is dressed with the utmost severity. Her face is pale and hard. DON LOPE goes up to her, full of attentions, and unwraps the scarf from his face.

DON LOPE eagerly: *Would you like us to go and have something to warm us up before we go home?*

TRISTANA does not reply. There is something absent and bizarre in her look. DON LOPE attracts her attention by laying his hand on hers.

TRISTANA brutally: *Leave me alone. I don't feel like talking.*

---

* Although the character pushing the wheelchair is given as Saturno in the original script, stills and the film itself seem to indicate that this is another character, possibly Vicente, the gardener.

She bangs her stick on the ground as a signal to SATURNO to move off. DON LOPE seems to become a little more bowed. Pan with them for a moment as SATURNO pushes the wheelchair along, escorted by DON LOPE and SATURNA. (Still on page 108)

High angle medium shot of a COMMANDANT of the *guardia civil* as he approaches from the opposite direction. He is a man of about forty, with a rather chubby but serious face. Camera tracks with him as he hurries forward to greet TRISTANA.

COMMANDANT: *Good morning, madam. Good morning, Don Lope.... To* DON LOPE: *You're still in fine fettle.*

TRISTANA nods amiably, while DON LOPE raises a hand to his beret.

COMMANDANT: *I see you're not afraid of the cold! ... As for the lady, I don't need to ask how she is, she could hardly look better.*

Close-up of TRISTANA.

TRISTANA: *That's very kind of you. Thank him, Lope.*

Camera tilts up to DON LOPE, who just manages a friendly smile. Pan to the COMMANDANT, then track back to show all three of them as he speaks. (Still on page 108)

COMMANDANT: *We intend to pay you a visit to thank you for the donation you've made to our orphanage; but this fortunate encounter enables me to express my personal gratitude.*

TRISTANA: *We only did our duty. When one is in a position to help others, then one has a duty to do so.*

COMMANDANT: *There are plenty of rich people, madam, but unfortunately donations such as yours are only too rare.*

He says goodbye with a cordial wave of the hand.

COMMANDANT: *Goodbye for now, Don Lope ... Madam ...*

TRISTANA nods in reply.

DON LOPE: *My respects, Commandant.*

The COMMANDANT salutes and goes out of shot.

Medium close-up of TRISTANA. She bangs on the ground with her stick.

TRISTANA: *Let's move!*

The little group goes on its way down the street.

The scene changes to the exterior of a country house, in the daytime. Situated not far from the town, it is a typical country dwelling, with a garden and a kitchen garden attached to the house. It is spring.

[VICENTE, the gardener, is working in the kitchen garden. A little farther away is another man, also working and bent forward so that we cannot see his face. VICENTE picks up a clod of earth and throws it at his assistant. The latter straightens up and turns round, and we recognise SATURNO, who grins interrogatively. The other man asks him in sign language for a cigarette. SATURNO goes over to him, takes out a cigarette, breaks it in two and gives half to VICENTE. They both light up.]*

The sequence begins with a low angle shot, showing the tops of the trees in the garden.

DON AMBROSIO off: *If your olive grove were well looked after, it would be one of the best around here.*

TRISTANA off: *Don't change the subject, Don Ambrosio.*

Camera tilts down to show a priest — DON AMBROSIO — and the gardener helping TRISTANA down some steps. She is wearing her artificial leg. She leans on DON AMBROSIO's shoulder, and the two of them advance slowly towards us, camera tracking out in front of them. (Production still on page 109)

DON AMBROSIO: *I have already told you all that I have to say. I think that in your case there's nothing more a priest can do. What you need . . .*

TRISTANA: *Don't talk to me about doctors. I need something else. . . .*

DON AMBROSIO: *As I've said to you many times, get married.*

TRISTANA: *How do you expect me to get married when you know quite well that I can't stand him?*

They walk off.

Medium shot: the two of them arrive at a garden seat and a chair. TRISTANA sits down. The priest draws up the chair and sits down facing her.

DON AMBROSIO: *And I say to you that you should overcome*

---

* This section was not shot.

this unhealthy sentiment. . . . When he really treated you badly you bore everything without saying a word, and now, just when he's treating you well . . . Why? . . . What more can you ask?

Camera tracks in slowly on Tristana. Her expression is very hard.

Tristana: *The better he treats me . . . the less I love him.*
Don Ambrosio: *But can't you see that's quite illogical?*
Tristana: *Perhaps, but that's how it is.*
Don Ambrosio off: *Take care, my child . . . there is something satanic in this resentment of yours.*

Tristana does not reply.

Medium close-up of Don Ambrosio.

Don Ambrosio: *I understand, you are young and he's . . . but since in your case the object of marriage would not be procreation but merely the sanctification of a situation which at present constitutes a . . . sin. . . . Well, you see what I mean.*

Towards the end of Don Ambrosio's speech, camera tracks back to show the two of them again. Seeing that Tristana is still silent, Don Ambrosio continues, taking off his hat.

Don Ambrosio: *Ask him to marry you and he'll accept, you'll see. You haven't noticed how he's changed! Old age is a great mellower . . . the corners get knocked off, one thinks differently.*

Track in to Tristana. Don Ambrosio continues off.

Don Ambrosio off: *He no longer forbids you to go to church, for instance. He even goes so far as to accompany you there!*

Tristana turns her head towards the house in the background.

Medium shot of what she sees: Don Lope comes out of the house carrying his coat and Tristana's walking-stick, camera panning with him.

Don Ambrosio off: *Marry him, my child. If you once had some affection for him, something must remain.*

Don Lope approaching: *I have to go into town, Don Ambrosio. If you've finished your business, I'll take you with me.*

The priest and Tristana can now be seen in the foreground.

Don Ambrosio: *With pleasure. . . . Thank you very much.*
Don Lope addresses Tristana, who does not even look at him. The gardener passes in the background.

Don Lope: *I'm going to the nursery to get some fruit trees. I'm taking the gardener. Is there anything you want?*

He gives the walking-stick to Tristana.

Tristana very curtly: *No, nothing.*

Don Lope: *Right, then.*

He bends down and is about to kiss her when Tristana throws an angry glance at him, indicating Don Ambrosio. Suddenly embarrassed, Don Lope moves away and takes the priest by the arm, as if this had been his intention all along.

Don Lope amiably, to the priest: *Right, let's be off.*

Don Ambrosio says goodbye to Tristana with a nod of his head, and the two of them move away, followed by Vicente, the gardener.

High angle medium close-up of Tristana. She gets up with a certain amount of effort, and camera pans as she makes her way slowly towards the house. She passes Saturno, who watches her go in then rinses his hands in a bucket of water.

General shot of Tristana's bedroom. She comes in and goes over to the bed, onto which she throws her walking-stick. Leaning against the end of the bed, she takes off her cardigan, then, hopping on one foot, she finally sits down on the edge of it. Camera tracks in slowly as she takes off her blouse.

Medium shot tracking in on Saturno as he walks past the front of the house eating some fruit. He looks up towards the window of Tristana's room. Camera tilts up, following his gaze.

High angle medium close-up of Tristana in her bedroom, now wearing a thin silk dressing gown. She is sitting in front of her dressing-table, brushing her blond hair, which falls to below her shoulders. She brushes it slowly, enjoying the sensation, but her movements are mechanical and her mind is elsewhere. Camera pans round the room to show her artificial leg lying on the bed. In the background the door opens noiselessly to reveal SATURNO. He comes in and bolts the door behind him, then comes towards TRISTANA. He places his hand gently on TRISTANA's shoulder, almost stroking it. TRISTANA turns towards him and makes negative gestures.

Medium close-up of SATURNO looking sheepish but excited. He explains to TRISTANA in sign language that he wants to go to bed with her.

Medium shot of the two of them. Furious, TRISTANA pushes his hand away. SATURNO seems distressed and, with more gestures, indicates that she must not say anything about his over-bold behaviour. (Still on page 109) He moves away and TRISTANA sits looking at her reflection in the mirror.

High angle shot of the garden near the house, beneath the window of TRISTANA's bedroom. SATURNO walks past looking sad, and bends down to pick up some gravel. Then he stands up again, looks up at the window and throws a piece of gravel at it. Camera pans and tilts up to show the window, keeping him in shot.

High angle close-up of the artificial leg lying on the bed in TRISTANA's bedroom. TRISTANA's hands appear in frame as they throw her underwear on top of it — first her slip, then her brassière and finally her knickers. Camera tilts up to show her closing the front of her dressing gown. Then she picks up her crutches from the end of the bed and goes towards the french window. (Still on page 110)

[High angle shot of SATURNO in the garden, as seen by TRISTANA. Sounds of birdsong. SATURNO looks up at the window in surprise.]*

Low angle reverse shot of the french window as it opens and TRISTANA comes out onto the balcony on her crutches. She looks down for a moment, while SATURNO looks up at her in the foreground, fascinated.

---

* This shot did not appear in the version screened.

High angle shot of TRISTANA, now seen from behind. SATURNO can be seen down in the garden in the background, gesturing to her and indicating in pantomime that she should open her dressing gown. He looks very excited.

Reverse angle medium close-up of TRISTANA. She opens her dressing gown in a haughty and imperious manner. (Still on page 110)

High angle shot of SATURNO, standing with his arms dangling at his sides, fascinated.

Resume on TRISTANA, as before, but now smiling.

Another high angle shot of SATURNO. The vision seems to be almost too much for him, and he retreats into the bushes, without lowering his eyes from the window. Camera tilts up over the greenery, while the birds sing merrily in the garden.

The scene changes to the interior of a church, where we see a highly ornamented statue of the Virgin, made of gilded wood, in low angle medium close-up.

Two more shots of similar statues.

General shot of the church; camera pans across to the altar, which is heavily ornamented. In front of it, facing camera, a priest — DON AMBROSIO — is blessing the bride and bridegroom.

DON AMBROSIO: *In the name of Our Lord Jesus Christ, go in peace . . .*

Camera tracks to give a better view of the couple, who have their backs to us. They are TRISTANA and DON LOPE, and near them are the witnesses, one of whom is DON COSME.

DON AMBROSIO: *. . . And may the Lord be with you always.*

He comes forward and kisses the hand of TRISTANA, who is dressed in black.

DON AMBROSIO: *Congratulations, Tristana. . . . And to you too, Don Lope.*

TRISTANA turns and picks up her walking-stick, then gets up and comes towards us, followed by DON LOPE. (Still on page 111) He tries to take her arm but she shakes him off irritably. Don Cosme follows, accompanied by a woman who is probably his wife. Camera moves with them as they pass in front of Saturna and Saturno; the two of them fall in behind the others. They all leave the church.

The scene changes to Don Lope's dining room, at night. Camera pans across the room to a medium shot of the table, on which can be seen the remains of a sumptuous meal. There are five places. In the centre of the table is a large wedding cake, a good quarter of which is missing. Two little figures representing the classic bride and bridegroom — she in a white dress and he in a tail coat — stand right on top of the cake. Saturna is clearing the table. She puts the glasses on a tray, empties all the dregs into one glass and then tastes the resulting mixture. She looks at the clock, which shows that it is around midnight. Suddenly she seems to remember something which she has forgotten to do, and camera pans with her as she goes rapidly out of the dining room and down the corridor towards Don Lope's bedroom.

[In the bathroom, we see Don Lope in his pyjamas, gargling. He sprays his mouth, then combs his hair.]*

Shot of the interior of Don Lope's bedroom. [The bed seen previously has disappeared, and has been replaced by an imposing canopied four-poster.]** Saturna appears and turns back the silk bed-cover to reveal linen sheets decorated with lace and embroidery. At the head of the bed are two pillows, also decorated with a profusion of lace. Saturna stretches and smooths the sheets, and plumps up the pillows. Camera pans as she goes to pick up another pillow, revealing Don Lope in his pyjamas, in front of the wardrobe. He goes towards the dressing-table and looks at himself in the mirror, puffing out his chest, then picks up an atomiser and carefully sprays his beard with perfume.

---

* Cut in the shooting.
** This piece of description is taken from the original script. In the film, the bed is in fact the same one as we have seen previously.

Medium shot looking down the corridor. TRISTANA appears, leaning on her stick, and advances slowly towards her room. On her way, she passes the open door of DON LOPE's room, where she stops and calls to him.

TRISTANA: *Lopito.* . . . He comes out and she says firmly: *Goodnight!*

DON LOPE is completely astonished. It is, after all, his wedding night, and he cannot understand his wife's attitude.

DON LOPE in amazement: *Where are you going?*

TRISTANA coldly: *To bed.*

DON LOPE: *What!* . . .

Surprise gives way to indignation. Clearly, DON LOPE has been nursing a number of illusions about the new state of affairs. Refusing to accept the situation, he appeals to her, while camera tracks in to show the two of them in medium close-up. He still has the atomiser in his hand.

DON LOPE: *But surely, tonight of all nights . . . You're not going to leave me all by myself?*

TRISTANA pretends not to understand his supplication. She goes to the door of her room and turns before going in. She scolds her husband like a child who has had a foolish idea.

TRISTANA: *After all.* . . . *You can't really think that at your age!* . . . *You're unbelievable!*

With a scornful laugh, she goes into her room and slams the door. Bowed and speechless with anger, DON LOPE goes back into his room, still clutching his atomiser.

Shot from inside DON LOPE's bedroom, with link on the motion as he comes in. SATURNA, who is still tidying a few things away, watches him; then she hurries diplomatically to the door.

SATURNA embarrassed: *Good night, sir.*

She goes out. Overwhelmed, DON LOPE goes and sits in an armchair beside a very luxurious footwarmer. He sits warming his hands.

The scene changes to the promenade in the town. We see in medium close-up the lottery wheel of the PEDLAR whom we saw earlier on in the film. TRISTANA's hand sets the wheel in motion.

PEDLAR off: *That's it, good and strong!*

Camera tracks back to reveal the PEDLAR seated facing us, with the wheel in front of him. SATURNO stands beside him on the left, while TRISTANA is seated in her wheelchair on the right. A small boy is watching them in the background.

PEDLAR: *Ten and five is fifteen, and three, eighteen . . .*

TRISTANA makes a sign to SATURNO and turns the wheel again.

PEDLAR: *. . . And three, twenty-one, and four . . . twenty-five it is!*

He stops the game and takes the lid off the canister on which the wheel is mounted, to reveal a stock of wafer cones inside.

Medium close-up of TRISTANA looking up at SATURNO. She has just taken the wafers she has won from the PEDLAR.

PEDLAR off: *Try your luck. . . . Wafers!*

SATURNO comes into shot, turns the wheelchair and pushes it away from camera.

Another shot of the public garden. DON COSME and a PRIEST walk forward and greet TRISTANA, who comes into view in her wheelchair, pushed by SATURNO. The PRIEST takes off his hat.

DON COSME: *How are you, Tristanita, well I trust?*

TRISTANA very drily: *How's your mother?**

DON COSME surprised and very embarrassed: *Very well, thank you.*

TRISTANA even more drily: *Me too, thanks! . . . Goodbye!*

---

* TRISTANA's riposte is more or less untranslatable, since in Spanish the phrase is highly insulting. According to Buñuel, in the past, to reply ' How's your mother? ' in an exchange of civilities such as this could provoke either a fight or a duel according to the circumstances.

She signals to SATURNO, who pushes her on again, while she eats the wafers which she has won from the PEDLAR. They go out of shot, watched in bewilderment by the PRIEST and DON COSME.

Another shot in the public garden. SATURNO continues to push TRISTANA along in the wheelchair, camera tracking out in front of them. Some members of the *guardia civil* can be seen in the background. SATURNO and TRISTANA pass a lady pushing a perambulator. TRISTANA casts a peculiar look at the pram and continues to munch her wafers. (Still on page 111) They go off and camera holds on a nursemaid sitting on a bench, rocking a baby in her arms.

The scene changes to DON LOPE's kitchen at night. We see SATURNA in medium shot, standing in front of the stove. She finishes heating some chocolate, then camera pans as she goes over to the table, where she pours the chocolate into a jug and sprinkles some sugar over some sugar cakes.

A shot down the corridor, where TRISTANA is seen walking on her crutches, away from camera. She is without her artificial leg. She passes SATURNA as the latter comes out of the kitchen and goes into the dining room, carrying a tray with the chocolate on it. TRISTANA turns round and starts walking back up the corridor again, camera tracking out in front of her. Her crutches sound loudly on the wooden floor. She comes into close-up, filling the screen.

High angle medium close-up of a priest — DON JOAQUIN — sitting at the table in the dining room, with a cup and saucer in front of him. He is leaning down and looking under the table; then he straightens up again.

DON JOAQUIN: *The brazier's just about right now.*
DON CANDIDO (another priest) off: *Isn't it cold today!*

Camera tilts up to show DON LOPE seated on the far side of DON JOAQUIN, unfolding a napkin. He is dressed in a thick dressing gown, with a beret on his head, and is wearing his glasses. He seems to have aged considerably.

Don Candido off: *My ears got absolutely frozen on the way here.*

Camera tracks out gradually to show first of all Don Ambrosio seated on the other side of Don Lope and then the third priest, Don Candido, seated opposite them. Saturna, who is standing in the background, fills their cups with chocolate. They also have a glass of milk each.

Don Lope: *As I was saying, I practically never set foot in the café these days. There's only two of us old 'uns left.*

Don Joaquin: *Well, I'm sure you'll bury the lot of them.*

Don Ambrosio: *We'll have our work cut out to outlast you.*

Don Lope pointing to his heart: *Don't you believe it, Don Ambrosio, don't you believe it! . . . After all the illnesses I've been through, the old ticker's not what it was. . . . And as for my blood pressure! . . .*

Don Candido: *Idle fears, Don Lope, idle fears! . . . The trouble is you're too pampered.*

Don Lope: *Excuse me a moment. I've forgotten my pills.*

He gets up, and camera pans as he goes off into the next room.

Resume on Don Candido and Don Ambrosio. They speak in low voices.

Don Candido: *If you ask me, he's sinking.*

They sit, contemplating their chocolate.

Medium shot, looking down the corridor. Tristana is still stumping up and down on her crutches.

Resume on the dining room. Camera tracks out gradually as Don Lope returns and sits down in his place between Don Ambrosio and Don Joaquin.

Don Lope: *My memory gets worse every day.* He holds up a pill. *I'm always forgetting them.*

Don Ambrosio: *Aha! Taking pills now, is he?*

Don Lope: *Would you pass the milk, please.* Don Joaquin hands him a jug. *Thank you.*

He pours himself some and drinks. We now see Don Candido in the foreground, drinking his cup of chocolate.

Don Joaquin: *What an aroma! Faced with such an exquisite beverage as this, how can we not pity those people who are*

forced to make do with tea?
DON LOPE: *I agree with you entirely.*
DON AMBROSIO: *Saturna is a great cook. Look how thick and creamy it is.*
DON JOAQUIN: *Just as it should be.*
> All four of them begin to sip the fragrant liquid. Outside, the wind whistles, while from the corridor comes the monotonous thump of TRISTANA'S crutches and her single foot.
> (Still on page 112)
> High angle medium close-up of DON AMBROSIO and DON CANDIDO, face to face.

DON AMBROSIO: *One seldom finds chocolate of this quality, is that not so, Don Candido?*
DON CANDIDO: *It is, I do confess. We are fortunate that Don Lope is so kind as to invite us here.* . . . He casts a reproachful glance at his colleague. *On the other hand, if the chocolate you have is not so good, it's no doubt because you prefer it that way.*
> Camera tracks out and moves round to include the other two men.

DON AMBROSIO: *My friend the archdeacon is no doubt hinting at the small private income left me by my poor parents.*
DON CANDIDO: *A small income? I'd be happy with half of it.*
DON LOPE: *Well now!* . . . *Do I gather that your salary is insufficient, Don Candido?*
DON CANDIDO: *We earn less than a bricklayer, Don Lope! And when one also has to support a widowed sister as I do, and the numerous nephews she has bestowed on me* . . .
> As they talk, they pass round the sugar cakes, which they dip in their glasses of milk.*
> Outside we see TRISTANA still continuing her monotonous progress up and down the corridor. She is scarcely thirty, but looks ten years older. She is dressed in black with a woollen jacket and a small scarf. Her dress is a modest one, but her face is luridly made-up and her expression is bizarre. She advances towards camera on her crutches

---

* These are in fact *azucarillos*, a kind of sugar bar made from sugar, white of egg and lemon juice, which is dipped in a beverage to sweeten it.

and it tracks out in front of her.

Resume on the table in the dining room. Don Lope is seen in profile, with Don Candido and Don Ambrosio in the background.

Don Ambrosio : *Come come, now, Don Candido, you mustn't start complaining, or Don Lope will think that we have an ulterior motive in coming to see him.*

Don Candido : *Our host knows very well that I am not in the habit of asking for anything for myself.*

Medium shot of the scene.

Don Lope : *I can testify to that.* He offers them some more chocolate : *Another cup, gentlemen?*

Don Joaquin : *Just half, thank you.*

Don Lope serves him, then there is a silence. Don Ambrosio dips a sugar cake in his milk. Don Joaquin drinks. Don Lope is happy; he enjoys watching his friends. He remains pensive for a moment, and then camera tracks in on him as he says, as if pursuing a line of thought :

Don Lope : *After all, gentlemen, life is not so black as a lot of people think. It's snowing good and hard outside . . . but in here we're warm and cosy.*

Reverse angle medium shot of the four of them at the table, with Don Lope in back view. Through the window in the background we can see the snow falling outside.

Rapid shot of the square outside, in the darkness. The snow is falling in large flakes.

Resume on the dining room. Camera tracks back from the window to show the room now in semi-darkness. The empty cups are still standing on the table. The cold has evidently penetrated the empty room. Camera pans towards the corridor, then into darkness.

The scene changes to Tristana's bedroom, at night. Tristana is in bed, once more having her nightmare. First we see a close-up of Don Lope's head as the clapper of the great bell, swinging to and fro. The mechanism creaks.

Medium shot of Tristana in her bed.
Don Lope off: *Tristana!* . . .
Camera tracks in as Tristana sits up in alarm and turns on her bedside lamp. The bell has disappeared. Tristana shivers. The choked voice of Don Lope is heard once more, calling from his room.
Don Lope off: *Tristana!* . . .
Tristana leans towards her crutches to get out of bed.
In his bedroom, Don Lope is lying in the darkness. His hand gropes around, trying to find the light-switch above the bed. He finally succeeds and turns it on, and we see him in high angle medium close-up. He apparently has a violent pain in his chest, and has great difficulty in breathing. He tries to call out again, but does not succeed immediately. A pause.
Don Lope: *Tristana! Tristana!*
He looks anxiously towards the door.* Camera pans and tracks round the bed as we hear the sound of Tristana's crutches off-screen. Then Tristana enters in the background, wearing a black shawl. She advances slowly towards the bed on her crutches and looks at Don Lope with a complete lack of expression.
Tristana: *What's the matter? Are you feeling ill?*
Don Lope nods. She sits down on the edge of the bed. He groans.
Tristana: *It must be something you ate at dinner.*
Don Lope shakes his head vigorously in denial.
Tristana very calm: *Do you want some lime tea?*
Camera tracks in again slightly.
Don Lope speaking with difficulty: *No, Tristana . . . this . . . is more serious. . . . I've got a pain . . .* He taps his chest *. . . here . . . it's killing me. . . . Call the doctor. . . . Quick!*
Tristana: *But . . . do you really feel as bad as that?*

---

* The original script had two extra shots inserted at this point, which were cut in the shooting:
'Resume on Tristana's bedroom. She has heard Don Lope's cries and is anxious. She gets up, puts a shawl round her shoulders and walks forward on her crutches.
'In the corridor, Tristana is seen going towards Don Lope's room.'

Don Lope: *Yes. . . . Call the doctor . . . please!*
He groans again — it is almost a death-rattle. Tristana gets up slowly and goes out on her crutches, into Don Lope's study.
Medium shot of Tristana as she goes towards the telephone in Don Lope's study and sits down. We are astonished by the slowness of her movements and her lack of expression. Camera tracks in on her as she sits and ponders. The opportunity is too good to be missed. At first she recoils at the idea of letting him die, but finally she makes a decision. She slowly picks up the receiver, but she does not put it to her ear, or dial a number. She hangs up again just as slowly, saying loudly as she does so:

Tristana: *Get me 240. . . . Doctor Miquis? It's me. . . . Yes, he's in a very bad way. . . . Good. . . . Come as soon as you can.* (Still on page 112)

She takes off the receiver and hangs up again noisily, then turns towards the door, as if listening to Don Lope's breathing. Her face expresses a state of patient, unhurried anticipation. The opportunity has arisen and she is taking advantage of it. That is all. Camera tilts with her as she gets up, picks up her crutches and goes out of the room.
Resume on Don Lope in his bedroom, panting weakly. His breathing is now no more than a kind of faint whistle. Camera pans to the open door as Tristana appears on her crutches, then follows her back again as she comes across to the bed. She looks down at the dying man and calls out in a low voice:

Tristana: *Lope!*

Don Lope's eyes are closed and he does not react. He is still panting, but more and more feebly.
Low angle shot of Tristana, leaning over the bed.

Tristana: *Lope! . . . Lope! . . . Doctor Miquis is coming straight away.*

There is no reply, only the sound of his breathing getting fainter and fainter. She leans towards him and shakes him.

Tristana: *Do you hear me, Lope? . . .* No reply. *Do you hear me?*

She looks towards the window, off-screen, then gets up.
Medium shot: TRISTANA moves round the bed and towards the window, camera panning with her. She opens both sides of the window and then goes out of shot. Camera holds on the open window: the snow is still falling outside; the wind whistles into the room.
Rapid shot of the small square outside; the snow is coming down thick and fast.
Medium close-up of TRISTANA as she leans over the bed and shakes DON LOPE, to make quite sure that he is dead. He does not react. A curious noise is heard, like a ringing in the ears or the whine of wind through telegraph wires; it gets louder and louder as the film draws to a close.*
Shot of TRISTANA at the telephone.
Shot of TRISTANA in her bed at night, in the middle of a nightmare. She sits up in a panic.
Close-up of the bell, with DON LOPE's head as the clapper.
The interior of the church: medium shot of the end of the marriage ceremony. Leaning on her stick, TRISTANA leaves the altar, followed by DON LOPE.
Shot of a statue of the Virgin, in the church.
TRISTANA's room in the country house, daytime: TRISTANA is seated at her dressing-table, with SATURNO standing behind her. He strokes her shoulder.
HORACIO's studio, daytime: medium close-up of TRISTANA and HORACIO, standing locked in a passionate embrace.
DON LOPE's living room, evening: medium close-up of DON LOPE and TRISTANA. DON LOPE is wearing a dressing gown. With his back to camera, he takes TRISTANA round the waist and leads her into his bedroom.
[An open space, daytime: medium close-up of TRISTANA and SATURNA, both dressed in black, with the HEADMASTER of the school for deaf-mutes, and SATURNO munching the apple which TRISTANA has given him. Then the two

---

* From this point on, the film consists of a series of rapid clips from the preceding scenes, moving backwards towards the beginning.

women walk away with their backs to camera.]*

Black screen: the words THE END come up, followed by the credits. The noise dies away.

---

* This last shot was not seen in the English version screened. However, the original script states emphatically: 'Repeat here sequence 1 of the scenario; the *only difference* should be that SATURNA and TRISTANA move away from the group instead of approaching it.'